December 1999-January, February

13 User-Friendly Bible Study Lessons
Based on the International Sunday School Lessons

BROADMAN COMMENTS
December 1999-January, February 2000

13 User-Friendly Bible Study Lessons
Based on the International Sunday School Lessons

ROBERT J. DEAN

JAMES E. TAULMAN

FRANK LEWIS

BROADMAN
& HOLMAN
PUBLISHERS

Nashville, Tennessee

© Copyright 1999 • Broadman and Holman Publishers
Nashville, Tennessee
All rights reserved

ISBN: 0-8054-1298-0

The Outlines of the International Sunday School Lessons, Uniform Series, are copyrighted by the Committee on the Uniform Series and are used by permission.

Broadman Comments
*is published quarterly
by Broadman & Holman Publishers,
127 Ninth Avenue, North, Nashville, Tennessee 37234*

The Scripture used is in the King James Version.

Dewey Decimal Classification: 268.61
Subject Heading: SUNDAY SCHOOL LESSONS—COMMENTARIES

ISSN: 0068-2721

POSTMASTER: Send address change to *Broadman Comments,*
Customer Service Center, 127 Ninth Avenue, North
Nashville, Tennessee 37234

Printed in the United States of America

WRITERS

STUDYING THE BIBLE

Robert J. Dean continues the theological traditions of *Broadman Comments* while adding his own fresh insights. Dean is retired from the Baptist Sunday School Board (now LifeWay Christian Resources) and is a Th.D. graduate of New Orleans Seminary.

APPLYING THE BIBLE

Frank R. Lewis is senior pastor of the First Baptist Church, Nashville, Tennessee.

TEACHING THE BIBLE

James E. Taulman is a freelance writer in Nashville, Tennessee. Prior to that, Taulman was an editor of adult Sunday school materials for the Baptist Sunday School Board (now LifeWay Christian Resources).

Contents

SECOND QUARTER
Studies in Matthew

UNIT I	**BEGINNINGS: BIRTH AND MINISTRY**
Dec. 5	— King's Herald and Baptism 3
Dec. 12	— Temptations and Ministry 11
Dec. 19	— Birth of Jesus 19
Dec. 26	— Coming of the Wise Men...................... 26

UNIT II	**JESUS' TEACHINGS AND MINISTRY**
Jan. 2	— The Disciples of Jesus 33
Jan. 9	— Teachings on Prayer.......................... 40
Jan. 16	— Miracles of Compassion 48
Jan. 22	— Opposition to Jesus 56
Jan. 30	— Laborers in the Vineyard 64

UNIT III	**FULFUILLMENT OF JESUS' MISSION**
Feb. 6	— Coming to Jerusalem 72
Feb. 13	— Watching for Christ's Return.................. 80
Feb. 20	— Death of Jesus 87
Feb. 27	— Resurrection and Commission................. 95

Studies in Matthew

December
January
February

1999—2000

INTRODUCTION

This study of Matthew's Gospel focuses on the life and ministry of Jesus. Most lessons depict a certain aspect of His ministry and how He was received by those to whom He ministered.

Unit I, "Beginnings: Birth and Ministry," is a four-lesson unit. The first lesson presents the preaching of John the Baptist and the baptism of Jesus. The second lesson looks at the temptations of Jesus and the beginning of His ministry. The third lesson is Matthew's account of the birth of Jesus, for the Sunday just before Christmas. The fourth lesson focuses on the coming of the wise men.

Unit II, "Jesus' Teachings and Ministry," is a five-lesson unit. Lessons include the calling and mission of the twelve disciples, teachings on prayer from the Sermon on the Mount, examples of Jesus' miracles of compassion, growing opposition to Jesus, and the parable of laborers in the vineyard.

Unit III, "Fulfillment of Jesus' Mission," is a four-lesson unit. These lessons focus on Jesus' royal entry and cleansing the temple, being ready for Christ's return, the death of Jesus, and the risen Lord's commission to His followers.

Cycle of 1998–2004

1998–1999	1999–2000	2000–2001	2001–2002	2002–2003	2003–2004
Old Testament Survey	Exodus Leviticus Numbers Deuteronomy Joshua	Judges 1, 2 Samuel 1 Chronicles 1 Kings 1–11 2 Chronicles 1–9	Parables Miracles Sermon on the Mount	2 Kings 18–25 2 Chronicles 29–36 Jeremiah Lamentations Ezekiel Habakkuk Zephaniah	James 1, 2 Peter 1, 2, 3 John Jude
New Testament Survey	Matthew	Luke	Isaiah 9; 11; 40–66 Ruth Jonah Nahum	Personalities of the NT	Christmas Esther Job Ecclesiastes Song of Solomon
John	1, 2 Corinthians	Acts	Romans Galatians	Mark	The Cross 1, 2 Thessalonians Revelation
Genesis	Ephesians Philippians Colossians Philemon	1 Kings 12– 2 Kings 17 2 Chronicles 10–28 Isaiah 1–39 Amos Hosea Micah	Psalms Proverbs	Ezra Nehemiah Daniel Joel Obadiah Haggai Zechariah Malachi	Hebrews 1, 2 Timothy Titus

December
January
February

1999–2000

THE GOSPEL ACCORDING TO MATTHEW

I. Beginnings: Birth and Ministry (Matt. 1:1–4:25)
   1. Genealogy and Birth of Jesus (1:1–25)
   2. Wise Men and Herod (2:1–23)
   3. John the Baptist and Jesus' Baptism (3:1–17)
   4. Temptations and Beginning of Ministry (4:1–25)
II. Ministry of the King-Messiah (Matt. 5:1–16:12)
   1. Sermon on the Mount (5:1–7:29)
   2. Miracles of Compassion and Power (8:1–9:34)
   3. Mission of the Twelve Disciples (9:35–11:1)
   4. Jesus Misunderstood and Rejected (11:2–12:50)
   5. Parables of the Kingdom (13:1–52)
   6. Mixed Responses to Jesus (14:1–16:12)
III. Mission of the Son of Man (Matt. 16:13–25:46)
   1. Revelation of the Way of the Cross (16:13–28)
   2. On and Off the Mount of Transfiguration (17:1–27)
   3. Teachings About Human Relationships (18:1–19:15)
   5. Royal Entry and Cleansing the Temple (21:1–22)
   6. Teachings in the Temple (21:23–23:39)
IV. Death and Resurrection of Jesus (Matt. 26:1–28:20)
   1. The Last Supper and Gethsemane (26:1–46)
   2. Betrayed, Arrested, Tried, Condemned (26:47–27:26)
   3. Crucified, Dead, and Buried (27:27–66)
   4. Great Commission of the Risen Lord (28:1–20)

King's Herald and Baptism

December 5 1999

Background Passage: Matthew 3:1–17
Focal Passages: Matthew 3:1–8, 11–17

Matthew 1–4 deals with "Beginnings: Birth and Ministry." Our "Studies in Matthew" will begin with the beginnings of Jesus' ministry, thus postponing studying the birth and the coming of the wise men for the Sundays before and after Christmas. This lesson deals with John the Baptist and with Jesus' baptism by John in Matthew 3.

▶**Study Aim:** *To explain the significance of John the Baptist's preaching and Jesus' baptism.*

STUDYING THE BIBLE

OUTLINE AND SUMMARY
  I. **John the Baptist (Matt. 3:1–12)**
    1. John preached repentance (3:1–6)
    2. John condemned religious leaders (3:7–10)
    3. John predicted baptism with the Spirit (3:11, 12)
  II. **Baptism of Jesus (Matt. 3:13–17)**
    1. Jesus explained why He was baptized (3:13–15)
    2. God showed His approval of His Son (3:16, 17)

John the Baptist preached repentance and baptized those who confessed their sins (vv. 1–6). He condemned the religious leaders for their dangerous hypocrisy (vv. 7–10). He predicted the coming of One who would baptize with the Spirit (vv. 11, 12). Jesus explained that His baptism was to fulfill all righteousness (vv. 13–15). The Father showed and spoke words that approved His Son's commitment to a mission as Suffering Servant (vv. 16, 17).

I. John the Baptist (Matt. 3:1–12)

1. John preached repentance (vv. 1–6)

  1 In those days came John the Baptist, preaching in the wilderness of Judaea,

  2 And saying, Repent ye: for the kingdom of heaven is at hand.

  3 For this is he that was spoken of by the prophet Esaias, saying, The voice of one crying in the wilderness, Prepare ye the way of the Lord, make his paths straight.

  4 And the same John had his raiment of camel's hair, and a leathern girdle about his loins; and his meat was locusts and wild honey.

  5 Then went out to him Jerusalem, and all Judaea, and all the region round about Jordan.

December 5, 1999

6 And were baptized of him in Jordan, confessing their sins.

These verses tell us the *who, when, where,* and *what* of the preaching of John the Baptist.

Who? By the time the Gospel of Matthew was written, the name and work of John the Baptist were so well-known that Matthew mentioned him with no introduction. His name came from his baptizing. The Jews had an immersion as one entry requirement for Gentiles who became Jews; however, John demanded that all needed to repent—Jews as well as Gentiles—as they confessed their sins.

The Jews had been expecting Elijah or a prophet like Elijah to precede the Messiah's coming (Mal. 4:5). When John emerged dressed in camel's hair and a leather girdle, they immediately thought of Elijah (2 Kings 1:8).

Matthew quoted Isaiah 40:3 as fulfilled in John the Baptist. John was the voice of the herald crying, "Prepare ye the way of the Lord." The symbolic picture of his work in verse 3 describes how special people went before a king announcing his coming and calling for the road to be made ready for him.

When? Unlike Luke, who gave the year in human history when John began his preaching (Luke 3:1), Matthew made only a vague reference to "those days." Matthew emphasized the time in God's epochs of His dealings with humanity, "The kingdom of heaven is at hand." Most Bible students recognize that "the kingdom of heaven" is the same as the "kingdom of God." The Jews, who had such great reverence for God's name that they wouldn't say it, often used "heaven" to refer to God. "Kingdom" here refers to the reign of God.

Jesus (Mark 1:14, 15) declared that the kingdom had arrived; but Jesus also taught His followers to pray, "Thy kingdom come" (Matt. 6:10). God has always been the Sovereign of all His creation, but people in their sins rejected His rule in their lives. The coming, life, death, and resurrection of Jesus declared the reality of that divine kingship and called people to accept God as King in their lives. For those who do, the kingdom becomes a reality in which we live by faith; but we also await the consummation of God's plan, when every knee will bow.

Where? John did his preaching "in the wilderness of Judaea." Strictly speaking, this is the barren area to the east of the Dead Sea; however, since John baptized people in the Jordan River, his area of ministry extended to the banks of the Jordan. The description in verse 5 has people coming to hear John from Jerusalem, Judea, and the region around the Jordan. Since John later got into trouble with Herod Antipas, who reigned over Perea (west of Jordan) and Galilee, John apparently at times preached on both the east and west sides of the Jordan River.

What? The preaching of John was basically a call to repent. The Greek word meant "to change one's mind," but actions as well as thoughts are changed in true repentance. To repent is to turn around and go in the other direction. (See Luke 3:10–14 for examples of specific changes that John called on people to make.)

A prominent feature in repentance is sincere confession of one's sins. Matthew does not emphasize John's baptism except as a call to and an occasion for confessing sins. Nowhere is there any hint that the waters of the Jordan washed away sins. God forgave sins as people confessed and forsook their sins (Ps. 32:5).

John the Baptist attracted a lot of attention for many reasons. People flocked out of Jerusalem, the farms and villages of Judea, and the regions all around the Jordan River. Some of them heeded his call and were baptized by John, confessing their sins.

2. John condemned religious leaders (vv. 7–10)

> **7 But when he saw many of the Pharisees and Sadducees come to his baptism, he said unto them, O generation of vipers, who hath warned you to flee from the wrath to come?**
>
> **8 Bring forth therefore fruits meet for repentance.**

Verse 7 introduces the Pharisees and Sadducees. They are listed together because members of these two major religious-political parties formed the Sanhedrin, the highest Jewish court in the land. Usually fierce enemies, these two groups formed a deadly alliance when anything threatened both of them.

John the Baptist saw these leaders among the crowd listening to his preaching. He knew they had not come to confess their sins. John the Baptist, like the Old Testament prophets, was never timid about condemning sin. Later his bold denunciation of Herod and Herodias led to his imprisonment and death (Mark 6:14–29). Jesus paid tribute to John as a courageous prophet (Matt. 11:7–15).

John called these self-important religious leaders a "generation of vipers." Like snakes, they dug their poisonous fangs into people. The religious leaders apparently at first tried to appear as part of the multitude of sincere seekers who came to escape divine wrath by confessing and forsaking their sin. John unmasked them. If they truly had come to repent of their sins, the fruits of sincere repentance were deeds of true righteousness. John knew that the leaders were trusting in their ancestry as descendants of Abraham, not in the transforming power of God (v. 9). The ax of divine judgment had already made its cutting mark on them; eventually God's wrath would fall (v. 10).

3. John predicted baptism with the Spirit (vv. 11, 12)

> **11 I indeed baptize you with water unto repentance: but he that cometh after me is mightier than I, whose shoes I am not worthy to bear: he shall baptize you with the Holy Ghost, and with fire:**
>
> **12 Whose fan is in his hand, and he will throughly purge his floor, and gather his wheat into the garner; but he will burn up the chaff with unquenchable fire.**

John contrasted his water baptism with the Spirit baptism of the One whose coming he preceded. Pentecost was the one-time historical fulfillment of the coming of the Spirit with power after the completion of Jesus' mission (Acts 1:5). The new birth when the Spirit comes into the life of a believer is its fulfillment in each Christian (John 3:1–8; Rom. 8:9).

December 5, 1999

John pictured himself as an unworthy servant compared to the Lord Jesus. He was not worthy even to carry His sandals. He was the Savior of penitent sinners and Judge of the impenitent. Verse 12 pictures the Lord as a farmer who separates the wheat from the useless chaff.

II. Baptism of Jesus (Matt. 3:13–17)

1. Jesus explained why He was baptized (vv. 13–15)

> **13 Then cometh Jesus from Galilee to Jordan unto John, to be baptized of him.**
>
> **14 But John forbad him, saying, I have need to be baptized of thee, and comest thou to me?**
>
> **15 And Jesus answering said unto him, Suffer it to be so now: for thus it becometh us to fulfil all righteousness. Then he suffered him.**

When Jesus came from his native Galilee, this was His first public appearance in preparation for launching His ministry. He asked to be baptized. However, John apparently recognized Jesus as the sinless One for whose coming he had been preparing the people. John, therefore, objected to baptizing Jesus. Instead, Jesus the sinless One should be baptizing John the unworthy servant.

Jesus' answer to John in verse 15, along with God's words from heaven in verse 17, are our best clues to why Jesus wanted to be baptized. Jesus had no sins to confess. Why then did He insist that John baptize Him?

For one thing, Jesus set an example for all who would later follow the Lord in the obedience of baptism. One meaning of "fulfilling righteousness" means to do the right thing by obeying God. Jesus obeyed the Father and was baptized; so do His followers obey the Father by being baptized as He commanded.

When taken with verse 17, verse 15 also pointed ahead to how Jesus would fulfill divine righteousness through His death and resurrection. Baptism depicts death and resurrection. At the beginning of His ministry, Jesus signified His commitment to a mission that would culminate in His death and resurrection. He was not one of the sinners who confessed their sins as John baptized them, but Jesus publicly identified Himself with these sinners, whom He had come to save.

2. God showed His approval of His Son (vv. 16, 17)

> **16 And Jesus, when he was baptized, went up straightway out of the water: and lo, the heavens were opened unto him, and he saw the Spirit of God descending like a dove, and lighting upon him:**
>
> **17 And lo a voice from heaven, saying, This is my beloved Son, in whom I am well pleased.**

Matthew emphasized that Jesus saw the Spirit descend on Him like a dove. Jesus was committing Himself to the mission given Him by the Father. The vision of the dove was the Father's assurance that the full power of His Spirit rested on Jesus.

The heavenly voice quoted parts of two important strands of Old Testament prophecy about the mission of the Messiah. The first part was from Psalm 2:7, which pictured the anointed One who would fulfill the royal role of Son of David and Son of God. The latter part was from Isaiah 42:1, one of Isaiah's Servant passages. The most explicit Servant passage is Isaiah 53—the Suffering Servant.

First-century Jews were looking for the Messiah-King, whom they expected to restore the power of Israel as it was in David's time. Few of them thought of Isaiah 53 as a prophecy of the Messiah. Jesus, however, saw the two as inseparable. He could become King only by way of the cross. He was committing Himself to this kind of mission. God's sign of the dove and the twofold reference to Psalm 2:7 and Isaiah 42:1 were the Father's stamp of approval on Jesus' commitment to a mission of salvation that involved suffering, death, and resurrection.

PRONUNCIATION GUIDE

Antipas	[AN tih puhs]
Esaias	[ih ZAY uhs]
Herod	[HAIR uhd]
Herodias	[hih ROH dih uhs]
Pentecost	[PEN tih kawst]
Perea	[puh REE uh]
Pharisees	[FER uh seez]
Sadducees	[SAD yoo seez]
Sanhedrin	[SAN he drihn]

SUMMARY OF BIBLE TRUTHS

1. All people need to confess their sins and turn from sin to God.
2. God's kingdom was revealed when Jesus came, but its consummation is still in the future.
3. Baptism with the Spirit took place historically at Pentecost and occurs personally when people experience the new birth.
4. Jesus committed Himself to a mission of death and resurrection.
5. At Jesus' baptism, God showed that this was the mission He had given His Son.
6. All believers should follow the Lord in baptism.

APPLYING THE BIBLE

1. How casually we use His name. We have come a long way from the days when God's name was revered. From the days of the Old Testament to the days when the Gospels were written, Jews went out of their way to avoid speaking the name of God for fear they would profane His holy name with human lips. They chose "kingdom of heaven" instead of "kingdom of God," "Adoni" or "LORD" instead of "Jehovah."

For many years we have lived in a culture that pairs the name of God with profanity and thinks nothing of it. Our conversation is marked like a pothole-scarred highway with casual expressions using God's name, slang expressions of Jesus, or the use of the word *holy* in ways that are anything but holy. It is a shameful loss of innocence that no one seems to notice.

2. Baptism as symbol. A young man made his profession of faith in our mission church in Nevada years ago. He was absolutely "broken" due to the regret of his wasted life. After talking with him about repentance and forgiveness, I felt he was ready for baptism. Just as we were about to enter the sanctuary, he turned to me and said, "Pastor, be sure to hold me under water just a little longer than usual. I've got lots of sin that has to be washed away."

What a comfort to remind him that the moment he asked Jesus to come into his life, all of his sin was washed away. We couldn't begin to stay underwater long enough to come up righteous, but thanks be to God, He has made us new creatures!

3. First impressions. We have often heard the phrase, "You only have one chance to make a good first impression." This causes us to develop a strong handshake, dress for success, read books on influencing others, strive for an impressive resume, act strong, give in to perfectionism, and often put on false airs that are intended to put us in enviable light in front of our peers.

Jesus made His first impressions in a totally different way. His earthly parents were humble, hard-working commoners. His birthplace was a stable. His first visitors were shepherds. Now, in His first public appearance beginning His ministry, Jesus identified with the outcast, the broken, the blind, the lost, those who were repentant and in need of a new beginning. He went to His cousin for baptism. This first impression of baptism marked the ministry of the Suffering Servant, born to die that we might die to live.

4. Baptism and obedience. If Jesus was willing to walk the estimated twenty-plus miles in the dangerous and difficult wilderness for a baptism that identifies Him with us (He who knew no sin with us who were lost and condemned in sin), what excuse can we possibly offer that justifies our disobedience?

5. Identifying an impostor. With the use of expensive, high-tech electronics and computer systems, security companies now have the ability to decrease the possibility of fraudulent access to high security areas they seek to protect. Body language takes on a whole new meaning these days. Fingerprinting software can correct or "heal" the intentionally altered imprint on the hands of a criminal. A machine that scans palm prints looks at two square inches in the center of the palm, and boasts a one-percent false reject and 0.00025-percent false acceptance rate. Machines that scan the human eye map the retina in a microsecond and can give positive identification with virtually no error.[1]

John the Baptist looked at the Pharisees and Sadducees, the religious leaders of the day, and spotted spiritual impostors immediately. Knowing they had not come to confess sin, he rejected them on sight, labeling them a "generation of vipers." Imagine how thoroughly God interprets the scan of our hearts.

6. Servant leadership. Jesus identified with John's ministry and man's need in His baptism. He modeled the role of Isaiah's Suffering

Servant and set the standard for those who would become His followers. Robert K. Greenleaf set the standard for servant leadership in business following his retirement when he wrote extensively on the subject. His ideas arose from his strong Quaker ethic. Walter Kiechel summarizes Greenleaf's philosophy with "The Five Things Every Servant Leader Does."[2]

- He takes people and their work seriously.
- He listens and takes his lead from the troops.
- He heals ("grief-work" is the new buzz word in consulting firms).
- He is self-effacing.
- He sees himself as a steward.

TEACHING THE BIBLE

- *Main Idea:* John's preaching and Jesus' baptism were evidences that God's kingdom had broken in on humans.
- *Suggested Teaching Aim:* To lead class members to identify how John's preaching and Jesus' baptism show how God broke through into human history.

A TEACHING OUTLINE

1. John the Baptist (Matt. 3:1–12)
2. Baptism of Jesus (Matt. 3:13–17)

Introduce the Bible Study

Use number 1, "How Casually We Use His Name," in "Applying the Bible" to introduce the lesson. Point out that Jesus and John took God's name seriously. Read aloud the "Main Idea" of the lesson and state that the lesson will help class members to identify why John's preaching and Jesus' baptism were significant.

Search for Biblical Truth

IN ADVANCE, enlist two people to read aloud the Scripture passages alternately—either every other verse or every other section.

To briefly overview the Scripture, write the five Scripture references of the background Scripture on a chalkboard or a large sheet of paper. Distribute paper and pencils and ask members to write a one-sentence summary for each reference. You could ask members to form five small groups of one or more persons and let each group write one summary or all members could write all five of the summaries.

Call on the members to read their summary of Matthew 3:1–6. On a chalkboard or a large sheet of paper, write: *Who? When? Where? What?* Ask members to open their Bibles to Matthew 3:1–12. Ask:

- Who is the subject of verses 1–6? (Write "John" opposite the word *Who?*)

December 5, 1999

- When did John begin his ministry? (Write "those days" opposite the word *When?* and use the information in "Study the Bible" to explain when "those days" were.)
- Where did John's preaching take place? (Write "wilderness of Judaea" opposite *Where?* Locate the area on a map showing Jesus' ministry.)
- What was the basic thrust of John's preaching? (Write "call to repent" opposite *What?*)

Call on the members to read their summary of Matthew 3:7–10. Ask members to suggest one-word descriptions of John's preaching. Ask, What two religious groups came to investigate John's preaching? (Pharisees and Sadducees.) What term did John use to refer to the religious leaders? (Vipers.) Why do you think this was an accurate term? What evidence of true repentance did John demand?

Call on the members to read their summary of Matthew 3:11, 12. Ask members to describe:

- John's attitude toward the Messiah;
- John's attitude toward himself; and
- What image John used to describe the way God was going to separate the evil from the righteous.

Call on the members to read their summary of Matthew 3:13–15. Using a map, locate Galilee and the approximate place on the Jordan River where John was baptizing (near Aenon—John 3:23). Using the material in "Studying the Bible," explain why Jesus insisted that John baptize Him.

Call on the members to read their summary of Matthew 3:16–17. Ask, What do you think the dove symbolized? Identify the two Old Testament Scriptures that the heavenly voice used. (Ps. 2:7 and Isa. 42:1.) Why do you think the heavenly voice quoted these?

Give the Truth a Personal Focus

IN ADVANCE, copy the six "Summary of Bible Truths" on six strips of paper and tape these to a focal wall. Ask members to explain how John's preaching and Jesus' baptism show how God broke through into human history. Ask members to suggest which statement applies most to them. Close in prayer.

---

1. Timothy O. Bakke, "Body-Language Security Systems," *Popular Science,* June 1996, 76.
2. Walter Kiechel III, "The Leader as Servant," *Fortune,* May 4, 1992, 121.

Temptations and Ministry

December 12 1999

Background Passage: Matthew 4:1–17
Focal Passage: Matthew 4:1–14

Two events involving Jesus Himself preceded the beginning of His public ministry: His baptism and His temptations. In our last study we focused on the preaching of John the Baptist, which led up to Jesus' baptism. In this lesson, we focus on the temptations of Jesus, which led to the opening part of His public ministry.

▶**Study Aim:** *To identify characteristics of temptation and ways to overcome temptation.*

STUDYING THE BIBLE

OUTLINE AND SUMMARY
 I. Temptations of Jesus (Matt. 4:1–11)
   1. Tested and tempted (4:1)
   2. Meeting physical needs (4:2–4)
   3. Using holy things (4:5–7)
   4. Achieving goals (4:8–10)
   5. Victory over temptation (4:11)
 II. Beginning the Galilean Ministry (Matt. 4:12–17)

Jesus was led by the Spirit into the wilderness, where He was tempted by the devil (v. 1). The tempter tried to get Jesus to use His power to meet physical needs (vv. 2–4). Jesus was tempted to rely on Psalm 91:11, 12 to save Him from harm (vv. 5–7). Then Satan tempted Jesus to achieve His goals without going to the cross (vv. 8–10). Jesus overcame temptation (v. 11). Jesus began His ministry where the people in darkness needed light (vv. 12–17).

I. Temptations of Jesus (Matt. 4:1–11)

1. Tested and tempted (v. 1)

1 Then was Jesus led up of the spirit into the wilderness to be tempted of the devil.

Temptation often strikes soon after a time of spiritual exaltation. "Then" shows that the wilderness experience came on the heels of the high moment for Jesus when the Spirit descended and the Father spoke His approval.

The Spirit led Jesus into the wilderness to be tempted by the devil. James 1:13–15 denies that God is tempted by evil or that God ever tempts anyone to do evil. The same Greek word can mean either "test" or "tempt." God leads us into situations in which our faith is tested, but His purpose is that our faith be strengthened. The devil, however, seeks to use such tests as temptations to do evil.

December 12, 1999

Hebrews 4:15 makes plain that Jesus was tempted as we are. Otherwise, He would not have been human as well as divine. Only as He faced and overcame real temptations was He enabled to be the sacrifice for our sins and to help us when we are tempted.

2. Meeting physical needs (vv. 2–4)

> **2 And when he had fasted forty days and forty nights, he was afterward an hungered.**
>
> **3 And when the tempter came to him, he said, If thou be the Son of God, command that these stones be made bread.**
>
> **4 But he answered and said, It is written, Man shall not live by bread alone, but by every word that proceedeth out of the mouth of God.**

One of the purposes for fasting in Bible times was to prepare for some special mission or experience (Exod. 34:28). As Jesus prepared to launch His public ministry, He went without food. Because Jesus had not eaten for so long, He was hungry. The devil, here called "the tempter," attacked at this point of meeting physical needs.

The form of the clause in Greek indicates that the word *if* meant "since." The tempter was not casting doubt on who Jesus was; he was challenging the Son of God to use His divine power to turn stones into loaves of bread. This was a temptation for Jesus on two levels. On a personal level, Jesus was tempted to use His power to perform a miracle to satisfy His own hunger. On another level, the devil was implying that Jesus could use His divine power to feed the starving people of the world.

He quoted Deuteronomy 8:3, which summarizes what God tried to teach the Israelites during their forty years in the wilderness (Deut. 8:2). As important as bread is to meet our bodies' needs for physical life, the Word of God is essential for the kind of deeper life that comes through faith in God.

People do not live by bread alone, but they do need bread. He taught us to pray for daily bread (Matt. 6:11). He taught us to feed hungry people (Matt. 25:31–46). At times Jesus did use His powers to feed hungry people (Matt. 14:13–21). However, because many of the Jewish people were expecting just such a messiah, when Jesus out of compassion fed five thousand people, they tried to make Him their kind of king (John 6:15). Jesus refused to be the kind of messiah they wanted (John 6:22–71).

Notice that Jesus quoted Scripture to turn aside the temptations. He practiced Psalm 119:11, "Thy word have I hid in mine heart, that I might not sin against thee."

3. Using holy things (vv. 5–7)

> **5 Then the devil taketh him up into the holy city, and setteth him on a pinnacle of the temple,**
>
> **6 And saith unto him, If thou be the Son of God, cast thyself down: for it is written, He shall give his angels charge concerning thee: and in their hands they shall bear thee up, lest at any time thou dash thy foot against a stone.**

7 Jesus said unto him, It is written again, Thou shalt not tempt the Lord thy God.

In the second temptation, Satan moved from the mundane to the holy. He took Jesus to the holy city and to the highest point on the holy temple. Then he quoted the holy Scriptures to Jesus to call on the holy God.

In rejecting the devil's temptation to turn stones into bread, Jesus had quoted holy Scriptures and even used a text that emphasized the Word of God. Picking up on that, the devil quoted Psalm 91:11, 12 as a basis for doing what he then asked Jesus to do. The devil implied: "All right, you want to obey the Holy Scriptures; Psalm 91:11, 12 is God's Word. It says to step out in bold faith and God will send His angels to deliver you. If that applied to any believer, how much more does it apply to You—since You are the Son of God?"

Like the first temptation, this was a temptation on two levels. On a personal level, the devil tempted Jesus to give God an opportunity to prove what He had said at Jesus' baptism. Words are one thing, the devil implied; but actions are another. By rescuing you from this fall, God will show beyond a shadow of a doubt that Jesus is His Son. On another level, Jesus was tempted to do something spectacular that would impress the people and gain Him a following immediately.

Jesus rejected the devil's interpretation of Psalm 91:11, 12. He saw that doing what the devil suggested would not be showing trust in God but putting God to the test. Thus, Jesus quoted Deuteronomy 6:16. God wants us to trust Him to care for our needs; and at times, God challenges us to launch out boldly on His Word alone. Testing is when we try to use God for our own purposes.

Jesus often used signs and wonders, but never to impress people and to gain an easy following from the fickle crowds. He resisted all demands for a sign to convince people (Matt. 12:38–42). He knew that people could see obvious signs and still refuse to believe (see Luke 16:29–31; John 11:44–53).

4. Achieving goals (vv. 8–10)

8 Again, the devil taketh him up into an exceeding high mountain, and sheweth him all the kingdoms of the world, and the glory of them;

9 And saith unto him, All these things will I give thee, if thou wilt fall down and worship me.

10 Then saith Jesus unto him, Get thee hence, Satan: for it is written, Thou shalt worship the Lord thy God, and him only shalt thou serve.

On the surface, this appears the most brazen temptation of all; but it was probably done more deceptively than it sounds. What kind of glory would tempt Jesus? He was not the kind of person who seeks worldly fame or pleasure. Jesus had been promised glory and the allegiance of the nations, but only after fulfilling His mission of suffering and death. Satan was probably offering Jesus a shortcut to achieving His mission. Satan suggested that he knew ways Jesus could accomplish His goals without all the suffering and without dying for sin.

The disciples often argued among themselves about human success and greatness. Jesus had to keep reminding them that His way involves humble, self-giving service—of which His death was to be the ultimate expression (Mark 10:35–45). People worship the devil when they adopt his methods of achieving their goals. People give in to the tempter's suggestion that the good end justifies whatever is necessary to achieve it. Those who look for the quick, easy way to achieve goals often are unknowingly bowing before the devil, whose first commandment is, "The end justifies the means."

5. Victory over temptation (v. 11)

11 Then the devil leaveth him, and, behold, angels came and ministered unto him.

The devil left him, but passages like Matthew 16:23; 26:36–46 show that Satan continued to tempt Jesus. However, Jesus had won a crucial victory over temptation. When the devil left, the angels came and ministered to Jesus. As in the case of Elijah, the ministry probably included feeding Jesus (1 Kings 19:5–8).

Jesus' victory shows several facts about temptation and how to overcome it. Being tempted is not the same thing as sinning. Jesus was tempted as we are; yet Jesus did not sin.

Temptation can be overcome. The devil could not force Jesus to sin. He cannot force any of us. He can tempt, but the one who yields to sin cannot blame Satan—as Eve tried to do (Gen. 3:13; see James 1:13–15).

God always provides a way to escape when we are tempted (1 Cor. 10:13). The resources that sustained Jesus are still available—the Word of God and the power of God's Spirit. In our case, the Spirit is the Spirit of the Lord Jesus, who knows what it is to be tempted as we are and who comes to encourage and empower us to overcome as He did (Heb. 2:17, 18; 4:14–16).

II. Beginning the Galilean Ministry (Matt. 4:12–17)

12 Now when Jesus had heard that John was cast into prison, he departed into Galilee;

13 And leaving Nazareth, he came and dwelt in Capernaum, which is upon the sea coast, in the borders of Zabulon and Nephthalim:

14 That it might be fulfilled which was spoken by Esaias the prophet.

John the Baptist's arrest, imprisonment, and execution are recounted later in Matthew (11:2; 14:1–12). Jesus had been brought up in the little town of Nazareth, which was in the larger area of Galilee. One of the key cities of Galilee was Capernaum, which was located on the northwest coast of the Sea of Galilee. Galilee was in the area of Canaan originally given to the tribes of Zebulun and Naphtali.

Focusing His ministry in Galilee fulfilled Scripture. John 7:41, 42 shows that most Judean Jews denied that the Messiah would come from Galilee. They no doubt were thinking of Micah's prophecy of the Messiah's birth in Bethlehem in Judea (Mic. 5:2; Matt. 2:5, 6). Matthew quotes Isaiah 9:1, 2 as being fulfilled in the ministry of Jesus in Galilee (4:15, 16).

The quotation shows why Jesus focused on Galilee. "Galilee of the Gentiles" (4:15) had more Gentiles than any other of the Jewish territories. Also the Galilean Jews were not well thought of by the more pious Jews of Judea, who lived nearer the holy city of Jerusalem. Jesus occasionally went to Judea. John's Gospel emphasizes His ministry in Judea and Jerusalem, but Matthew emphasizes His work in this area of moral and spiritual darkness. He brought light to the Jews of Galilee during His earthly ministry, but His ministry in Galilee foreshadowed the worldwide scope of the gospel after Pentecost.

Jesus began preaching the same message that John the Baptist preached (compare 4:17 and 3:2).

PRONUNCIATION GUIDE

Capernaum	[kuh PURR nay uhm]
Esaias	[ih ZAY uhs]
Galilee	[GAL ih lee]
Nazareth	[NAZ uh reth]
Nephthalim	[NEF thuh lim]; same as Naphtali [NAF tuh ligh]
Zebulun	[zeb YOO luhn]; same as Zabulon

SUMMARY OF BIBLE TRUTHS

1. God allows us to be tested, but the devil tempts us to do evil.
2. Because Jesus was tempted as we are, yet without sinning, He is able to help us overcome temptations.
3. The devil uses every trick in his trade, including quoting Scripture.
4. Jesus relied on the Scriptures and the Spirit to overcome temptation.
5. The devil can tempt us, but each of us is responsible if we yield to temptation and sin.
6. Jesus shines His light where moral and spiritual darkness are greatest.

APPLYING THE BIBLE

1. Spiritual challenges and temptation. In a recent survey of *Discipleship Journal,* readers ranked areas of greatest spiritual challenge to them:
- materialism,
- pride,
- self-centeredness,
- laziness,
- anger/bitterness,
- sexual lust,
- envy,
- gluttony, and
- lying.

Survey respondents noted temptations were more potent when they had neglected their time with God (81 percent) and when they were physically tired (57 percent). Resisting temptation was accomplished by prayer (84 percent), avoiding compromising situations (76 percent), Bible study (66 percent), and being accountable to someone (52 percent).

2. Repeated battles. "You may have to fight a battle more than once to win it" (Margaret Thatcher).

3. Excuses. We live in a society where excuses for immoral behavior abound. Think of the Old Testament character, Joseph. When Potiphar's wife invited him to become her "lover," Joseph could have offered any one of the following excuses to rationalize his sin. He could have said:

- "It's only natural to do this. After all, God gave me the physical desire."
- "I'm lonely, and this is a way to satisfy a God-given need that I have."
- "I've had a hard life of rejection from my family, and I owe this to myself."
- "I'm different from others; this won't affect me or my walk with God in the long run."
- "It's not all my fault. I'm just a slave. I have to do what she says."
- "The palace is empty. I can do this and no one will ever know about it."

Yes, Joseph could have offered any one of these excuses. But he didn't. The appeals were many. Going to bed with Potiphar's unfaithful wife probably appealed to Joseph physically, mentally, emotionally, and even spiritually. ("Where was God when I was sold into slavery?" Joseph could have asked.) In the end, he demonstrated the best way for us to avoid sin in the midst of temptation. He ran the other way! (See Gen. 39:1–12.)

4. The character of temptation. Temptation can be explained by making an acrostic from the word to teach significant truths from today's lesson. One acrostic may include the following phrases.

T	Temptation is an invitation to sin, but it is not a sin to be tempted.
E	Temptation often says, "The end justifies the means."
M	Temptation causes us to mistrust in the provision and promises of God.
P	Temptation appeals to the passions you cultivate in your life. (If you have a problem with lust, quit watching explicit material on TV and memorize Job 31:1.)
T	The timing of temptation often follows periods of spiritual growth.
A	God is faithful and always provides a way of escape.
T	Tests and trials are the very fabric of faith.
I	Temptation is an invitation to grow stronger or weaker spiritually, depending on our response.
O	Overcoming temptation requires discipline.
N	No one is immune to being tempted. No one.

5. What would you do? F. B. Meyer is credited with saying, "When we see a brother or sister in sin, there are two things we do not know:

First, we do not know how hard he or she tried not to sin. And second, we do not know the power of the forces that assailed him or her." Stephen Brown adds, "We also do not know what we would have done in the same circumstances" (Stephen Brown, *Christianity Today,* April 5, 1993, 17).

6. Avoid the temptation. This poem speaks to the human nature of putting ourselves in the path of temptation. It ends by reminding us how to avoid temptation traps in the future.

There's a Hole in My Sidewalk

I walk down the street.
There is a deep hole in the sidewalk.
I fall in.
I am lost . . . I am helpless, it isn't my fault.
It takes forever to find a way out.
I walk down the same street.
There is a deep hole in the sidewalk.
I pretend I don't see it.
I fall in, again.
I can't believe I am in the same place.
But, it isn't my fault.
I walk down the same street.
There is a deep hole in the sidewalk.
I see it there.
I still fall in . . . it's a habit . . . but I know where I am.
It is my fault.
I get out immediately.
I walk down the same street.
There is a deep hole in the sidewalk.
I walk around it. I walk down another street.

—Portia Nelson

TEACHING THE BIBLE

▶ *Main Idea:* Jesus used Scripture and His relationship with God to overcome temptation.
▶ *Suggested Teaching Aim:* To lead adults to identify ways Jesus overcame temptation.

A TEACHING OUTLINE

1. *Temptations of Jesus (Matt. 4:1–11)*
2. *Beginning the Galilean Ministry (Matt. 4:12–17)*

Introduce the Bible Study

Use number 1, "Spiritual Challenges and Temptation," in "Applying the Bible" to introduce the lesson.

December 12, 1999

Search for Biblical Truth

IN ADVANCE, number the summary statements in "Outline and Summary" and copy them on six small strips of paper. Give the statements to six different members. Ask the person with the first strip to read it aloud and read Matthew 4:1. Briefly lecture concerning the following points:

- Temptation often strikes soon after a time of spiritual exaltation.
- Locate the "wilderness" on a map of Jesus' ministry.
- The role of the devil and the Spirit in the temptation.

DISCUSS: Why do you think that temptation often strikes so close to times of spiritual high?

Ask the person with the second summary strip to read it aloud and then read Matthew 4:2–4. Ask: What did the tempter ask Jesus to do in these verses? Why do you think this was a real temptation for Jesus? What were the two levels of temptation for Jesus? How did Jesus respond?

DISCUSS: Why, when we have power to provide bread for hungry people, are we tempted to keep it for ourselves?

Ask the person with the third summary statement to read it aloud and to read Matthew 4:5–7. Ask: What did the tempter ask Jesus to do in these verses? Why do you think this was a real temptation for Jesus? What were the two levels of temptation for Jesus? How did the tempter misquote Scripture? How did Jesus respond?

DISCUSS: What are some examples today of people who are still trying to appeal to the spectacular by performing signs and wonders?

Ask the person with the fourth summary statement to read it aloud and to read Matthew 4:8–10. Ask: What did the tempter ask Jesus to do in these verses? What was the likely meaning of this temptation for Jesus? Why do you think this was a real temptation for Jesus? How did Jesus respond?

DISCUSS: What are some ways we give in to this temptation today?

Ask the person with the fifth summary statement to read it and Matthew 4:11 aloud. Read the three statements in "Studying the Bible" in the commentary on verse 11. Ask members if they agree or disagree with the following statements:

- "Being tempted is not the same thing as sinning."
- The devil "can tempt, but the one who yields to sin cannot blame Satan—as Eve tried to do."
- "God always provides a way to escape when we are tempted."

Ask the person with the sixth summary statement to read it and Matthew 4:12–17. Locate Galilee on the map and show where Jesus went when John was arrested.

DISCUSS: How would you compare and contrast Jesus' preaching with John the Baptist's preaching?

Give the Truth a Personal Focus

Use the summary statements to present a brief lecture summarizing the truths of the lesson. Close in prayer.

Birth of Jesus

December 19, 1999

Background Passage: Matthew 1:1–25
Focal Passages: Matthew 1:1–6, 18–25

Matthew 1–2 and Luke 1–2 describe the events related to the birth of Jesus. John 1:1–18 provides a theological perspective. Jesus is the focus in all these Gospels; however, Matthew tells the story from Joseph's point of view, and Luke, from Mary's. Matthew 1 tells of the genealogy of Jesus and of the announcement of His birth to Joseph.

▶**Study Aim:** *To testify to what Matthew 1 says about who Jesus is and what He came to do.*

STUDYING THE BIBLE

OUTLINE AND SUMMARY
  I. Genealogy of Jesus (Matt. 1:1–17)
 II. Announcement of the Birth of Jesus (Matt. 1:18–25)
      1. Joseph and Mary (1:18, 19)
      2. Jesus Immanuel (1:20–23)
      3. Joseph's trust and obedience (1:24, 25)

The genealogy of Jesus presents Jesus as the Messiah-King who fulfilled God's promises to David and as One who came for all people (vv. 1–17). Jesus is central, but God chose two people of genuine faith to raise Him (vv. 18, 19). Jesus is the incarnate Son of God and Savior from sin, who came into the world by means of a miraculous conception to a virgin (vv. 20–23). Joseph acted with complete trust and obedience to the Lord (vv. 24, 25).

I. Genealogy of Jesus (Matt. 1:1–17)

1 The book of the generation of Jesus Christ, the son of David, the son of Abraham.

2 Abraham begat Isaac; and Isaac begat Jacob; and Jacob begat Judas and his brethren;

3 And Judas begat Phares and Zara of Thamar; and Phares begat Esrom; and Esrom begat Aram;

4 And Aram begat Aminadab; and Aminadab begat Naasson; and Naasson begat Salmon;

5 And Salmon begat Booz of Rachab; and Booz begat Obed of Ruth; and Obed begat Jesse;

6 And Jesse begat David the king; and David the king begat Solomon of her that had been the wife of Urias.

Beginning a book with a long genealogy seems strange to us today; however, genealogies are a familiar feature in the Old Testament; and this particular genealogy reveals much about who Jesus is and what He came to do.

Jesus was the fulfillment of Old Testament promises. "The book of the generation" reminds us of similar words that separate the divisions of the

December 19, 1999

Book of Genesis (see for example, Gen. 2:4; 5:1; 6:9; and so on). The name or title "Christ" means "Anointed One" and refers to the Messiah-King for whom the Jews looked, based on God's covenant with David (2 Sam. 7:11b–16). Thus Jesus (Savior, see 1:21) Christ was the son of David. The arrangement of the names in the genealogy emphasizes Jesus as the son of David. Verses 2–6 go from Abraham to David; verses 7–11 go from David to the exile, which seemed the end of David's line of kings; however, 12–16 go from the exile and show that Jesus was the true King.

Jesus also was the son of Abraham. He fulfilled God's promises to Abraham (Gen. 12:1–3), which were renewed with the other patriarchs Isaac and Jacob. Jacob predicted that the Promised One would come from the tribe of Judah, David's tribe (sometimes spelled "Judas"; Gen. 49:10).

The unusual feature of this genealogy is the mention of five women: Tamar (Thamar), Rahab (Rachab), Ruth, wife of Uriah (Bathsheba), and Mary. Tamar was the daughter-in-law of Judah, whose husband had died before she bore children; therefore, she disguised herself as a prostitute in order to have a child by Judah (Gen. 38). Rahab was the prostitute of Jericho whose family was spared because she hid the Israelite spies (Josh. 2). We are more familiar with the other three. Why did Matthew depart from custom by adding the names of these women?

As far as the first four are concerned, they were probably added to remind readers of the inclusiveness of Jesus' mission. He came for women as well as men. He came for Gentiles as well as Jews (Rahab and Ruth were foreigners). He came to save sinners. Tamar, Rahab, and Bathsheba were involved in sexual sins. If we are looking for sinners, we can also find many among the male ancestors of Jesus, including David himself. The most notorious sinner in the list was King Manasseh (v. 10).

Mary is included because she was the mother of Jesus. Although the genealogy was based on the line of Matthew, verse 17 sets the stage for the description of the miracle of Jesus' conception by the Holy Spirit (v. 20) and His birth to a virgin (vv. 22, 23).

II. Announcement of the Birth of Jesus (Matt. 1:18–25)

1. Joseph and Mary (vv. 18, 19)

18 Now the birth of Jesus Christ was on this wise: When as his mother Mary was espoused to Joseph, before they came together, she was found with child of the Holy Ghost.

19 Then Joseph her husband, being a just man, and not willing to make her a publick example, was minded to put her away privily.

Although the focus in Matthew 1 is on Jesus, some attention is given to the kind of people God chose to raise Him. Luke 1:26–38 tells of the angel's announcement of Jesus' birth to Mary, a dedicated, obedient, pure young woman of simple yet profound faith and trust in God. She and Joseph were engaged but not yet married. First-century Jewish engagements were more binding than modern engagements. A formal agreement or contract bound them to become married. This relationship could be broken only by a divorce.

In those days, as should be true in every generation, the engaged couple did not engage in sex. That came only after they were married. Although Joseph is called Mary's "husband," the word *espoused* refers to being engaged; and the words *before they came together* emphasize that they were not living together as husband and wife.

During this period, Joseph became aware that Mary was expecting a child. The Bible does not tell us whether Mary had told Joseph of the unique manner of the child's conception. My own feeling is that she had not told him. For one thing, Mary was a person of trust, and she probably trusted God to inform Joseph in His own way and time. In addition, the actions of Joseph strongly imply that he did not know she was pregnant until it became apparent that she was.

The custom of the day was for the man to subject his unfaithful fiancee to divorce and public humiliation. Joseph chose not to do this. He is described as "a just (righteous) man." He did not want a wife who was guilty of adultery, but he was not a vindictive man. Mercy tempered his sense of doing what was right. Therefore, he made plans to divorce Mary but to do so as quietly as possible. He felt this would be best for all concerned—himself, Mary, and the child.

2. Jesus Immanuel (vv. 20–23)

20 But while he thought on these things, behold, the angel of the Lord appeared unto him in a dream, saying, Joseph, thou son of David, fear not to take unto thee Mary thy wife: for that which is conceived in her is of the Holy Ghost.

21 And she shall bring forth a son, and thou shalt call his name JESUS: for he shall save his people from their sins.

22 Now all this was done, that it might be fulfilled which was spoken of the Lord by the prophet, saying,

23 Behold, a virgin shall be with child, and shall bring forth a son, and they shall call his name Emmanuel, which being interpreted is, God with us.

Mary's confident trust in God was justified. God sent an angel to speak to Joseph in a dream and to tell him what an angel had told her months before. Mary was not guilty of adultery; the child was miraculously conceived by the Holy Spirit. Neither in this announcement to Joseph nor in the announcement to Mary is this miracle described in sensual terms, like the pagan myths of gods who cohabited with humans. Yet it was a miracle involving conception without a human father.

Joseph and Mary were both told to name the child Jesus. Joseph was told why. Names in those days had great significance. The name *Jesus* means "the Lord (Yahweh or Jehovah) is Savior." The mission of Jesus was to save people from their sins. This reinforces the implication of including the names of sinners in the genealogy.

The miraculous conception of the Savior fulfilled Old Testament prophecy. Matthew quoted Isaiah 7:14, which foretold the virgin birth of One called Immanuel (Emmanuel). Matthew explained to any non-Jewish readers that this name means "God with us." What more appropriate way for the incarnate Son of God to enter the world on His mission as Savior?

December 19, 1999

The miraculous conception of Jesus is only one of a number of events that point to this great miracle of incarnation. The doctrine of incarnation emphasizes that the eternal Word or Son of God became "flesh" (a real human being; see John 1:1, 2, 14). The events described in Matthew 1–2 and Luke 1–2, which we tell and retell each Christmas, emphasize both the human and the divine in the coming of the Savior. It was as if heaven came down and touched earth in this mixture of the heavenly and the earthly.

The earthly is seen in such things as shepherds tending their flocks, a young woman giving birth in humble surroundings, wise men searching the heavens for a sign. The heavenly is seen in the sudden appearance of angels to announce a special birth to the shepherds. It is seen in the miraculous conception of the child; although the birth was real enough in physical terms, the young mother was a virgin. It is seen in a miraculous star that led the wise men to where the young child was in order that they might worship Him.

The miracle of Jesus' conception fits the entire miracle of all the events of His coming, His ministry, His death, His resurrection, and His continuing work through the Spirit. Anyone who believes in the God of creation and redemption believes in a God who has acted in ways beyond human understanding to bring sinners to Himself.

3. Joseph's trust and obedience (vv. 24, 25)

> **24 Then Joseph being raised from sleep did as the angel of the Lord had bidden him, and took unto him his wife:**
>
> **25 And knew her not till she had brought forth her firstborn son: and he called his name JESUS.**

We honor Mary for her trust and obedience. Joseph showed the same kind of trust and obedience. He did not question the angel's unusual (to say the least) explanation for Mary's pregnancy, nor did he delay in obeying what the Lord told him to do. Instead of divorcing Mary, he married her. However, he carefully refrained from any sexual relations with her until after she had borne her firstborn son. When the child was born, Joseph named Him Jesus—as the angel had told him to do.

Luke 2:1–7 tells more details of the events connected with the actual birth. Matthew 1:25 simply tells us that this incarnate Savior was born to the virgin Mary.

Those who know Jesus Christ as Lord and Savior are able to show the kind of trust and obedience seen in Joseph and Mary—and thus to experience the true meaning and joy of celebrating Christmas.

PRONUNCIATION GUIDE

Aminadab	[uh MIN uh dab]
Aram	[AY ram] same as Ram
Booz	[BOH ahz] same as Boaz
Esrom	[ES ruhm]
Naasson	[nay ASS uhn]
Phares	[FAY reez] same as Perez
Rachab	[RAY kab] same as Rahab
Thamar	[THAY mar] same as Tamar
Zera	[ZEE ruh] same as Zerah

SUMMARY OF BIBLE TRUTHS

1. Jesus is the Messiah promised in the Old Testament.
2. He came as Savior for all kinds of people.
3. God chose two people of genuine faith to raise His Son.
4. Jesus is the One whom God sent to save people from their sins.
5. His conception by the Holy Spirit and His birth to a virgin are consistent with the total miracle of salvation.
6. Only those who know Jesus as personal Savior and Lord can understand the real meaning and joy of Christmas.

APPLYING THE BIBLE

1. A child's complete Christmas. A young girl slipped a piece of paper into her pastor's hand just as he was entering the sanctuary for the Christmas Eve service. As he sat down, he unfolded the paper and read the precious words that express the true joy of Christmas written in her simple handwriting.

Katherine Hall's Complete Christmas Recipe[1]

½	cup of joy
4 ½	cups of peace
2	cups of love
3 ⅓	cups of praise
7	cups of Christ
5 ¾	teaspoons of giving

Stir gently for 1 minute.
Share with others the true Christmas.

2. Gifts of Christmas:

God's gift:	Jesus
Joseph and Mary's gift:	obedience
The shepherds' gift:	wonder
The wise men's gift:	excellence
Jesus' gift:	peace

3. The gift goes on, but only if delivered. Margaret Taylor died three weeks before Christmas without getting a chance to mail the Christmas cards and wrapped presents that sat on a table in her home. But the police officer who found the 77-year-old woman's body made sure the gifts and cards were sent. Officer Aisha Perry stamped the cards and mailed them along with the packages, including a note telling Ms. Taylor's friends that she had died.

Since then, ten people have written the officer to thank her for the cards and tell her stories about their old friend. The gifts brought joy to those for whom they were intended and to the one committed to seeing that they were delivered.

The message of Christmas is a gift that keeps on giving, too, but it has to be delivered. Jesus is the source of joy, and those who know Him can't help but share the message with those who don't.

December 19 1999

4. Joy. Joy shared is joy doubled.

5. No presents, but a wonderful gift. In the classic tale *Little Women* (1868), Louisa May Alcott brought the story of her past to life. Facing the hardship of a nation rebuilding following the Civil War, she wrote, "Christmas won't be Christmas without any presents."

But God has given the greatest gift through His Son Jesus. There will always be a gift available to us because of what Christ accomplished on our behalf.

6. The greatest gift:
GOD: the greatest Lover
SO LOVED: the greatest degree
THAT HE GAVE: the greatest act
HIS ONLY BEGOTTEN SON: the greatest gift
THAT WHOSOEVER: the greatest opportunity
BELIEVETH: the greatest simplicity
IN HIM: the greatest attraction
SHOULD NOT PERISH: the greatest promise
BUT: the greatest difference
HAVE: the greatest certainty
EVERLASTING LIFE: the greatest possession.

7. Letters to Santa. We often read "Letters to Santa" from children. Adults have been known to write them, too:

> Dear Santa,
> Christmas Eve I'll be 46. I'm in great need of eyeglasses. I cannot see to read any more. I live in the hills of Appalachia and with no work here, there's no money for such things. If you could find me glasses, I'd be ever grateful.
>
> Shirley, from Kentucky[2]

Jesus did not come to be the world's Santa, but He did come to be the Light of the world. Those walking in darkness, the prophets cried, upon them a light will fall. Until all the Shirleys in the world have their spiritual sight restored—our task in sharing the gift of Christmas—the message of Christ is not complete.

TEACHING THE BIBLE

- *Main Idea:* Jesus is God's Son and came to save the world from sin.
- *Suggested Teaching Aim:* To lead adults to demonstrate the same kind of trust and obedience seen in Joseph and Mary.

A TEACHING OUTLINE

1. *Genealogy of Jesus (Matt. 1:1–17)*
2. *Announcement of the Birth of Jesus (Matt. 1:18–25)*

Introduce the Bible Study

Use No. 3, "The Gift Goes On," in "Applying the Bible" to introduce the lesson. Point out that Jesus' birth was God's eternal and everlasting gift to the world.

Search for Biblical Truth

On a chalkboard write in two columns: *Known* and *Unknown.* Ask members to open their Bibles to Matthew 1:1–6 and identify people in Jesus' genealogy whom they know. List these under *Known.* List all the others under *Unknown.* Now ask members to identify the women in Jesus' genealogy. (Tamar, Rahab, Ruth, and Bathsheba.) Ask: Why was it unusual to include women in a genealogy? What is unusual about these women that would link them all together? (They were either foreigners [Ruth, Rahab] or had sexual sin in their background [Rahab, Tamar, Bathsheba] or both [Rahab].)

IN ADVANCE, assign someone a three- to four-minute report on the four women in Jesus' genealogy. Call for the report at this time. Ask: Why do you think Matthew included these particular four women in his listing of Jesus' ancestors? Let members share their answers. Include the following: Jesus came for women as well as men; He came for Gentiles as well as Jews; He came to save sinners.

DISCUSS: What does Jesus' genealogy say to us about our ancestry?

On a chalkboard write *Joseph* and *Mary.* Ask members to locate Matthew 1:18–19 and list characteristics of these two people whom God had chosen to raise His Son. Use the material in "Studying the Bible" to explain first-century engagement/marriage customs.

Ask members to look at Matthew 1:20–23 and answer these questions: What were Mary and Joseph to name the child? Why did Jesus come? What prophet did Matthew cite who had predicted Jesus' birth? What name did Isaiah give the child?

Point out that Jesus' birth was a mixture of the heavenly and the earthly. On the chalkboard, write *Heavenly* and *Earthly.* Ask members to suggest the heavenly events associated with Jesus' birth. (Your members may think of others but consider: angels, miraculous conception, and miraculous star.) Now ask members to suggest earthly events. (Shepherds, young woman giving birth, wise men.)

Ask members to look at Matthew 1:24–25. Ask, How did Joseph display trust and obedience? (Did not question angel; married Mary immediately; named the Baby Jesus.)

Give the Truth a Personal Focus

Write the six "Summary of Bible Truths" statements on small strips of paper. Distribute these and ask members to: (1) read aloud the statement and (2) suggest one way that truth will apply to their life this coming week.

IN ADVANCE, copy the following quotation on a large poster and display it at this time: "Those who know Jesus Christ as Lord and Savior are able to show the kind of trust and obedience seen in Joseph and Mary—and thus to experience the true meaning and joy of celebrating."

---

1. Katherine Hall, First Baptist Church, Nashville, Tennessee, Christmas Eve 1997.
2. *Good Housekeeping,* Dec. 1994, 74.

December 26 1999

Coming of the Wise Men

Background Passage: Matthew 2:1–23
Focal Passage: Matthew 2:1–12

Matthew 2 tells of two kinds of people who both claimed to want to worship Jesus. The wise men sought Him sincerely. Herod sought Him insincerely. The wise men, on whom this lesson focuses, found Jesus and worshiped Him. God delivered Jesus from the evil, deceitful Herod; and God even used the wise men to help thwart the evil plans of Herod.

▶**Study Aim:** *To recognize the significance of the coming of the wise men.*

STUDYING THE BIBLE

OUTLINE AND SUMMARY

I. **Seeking Jesus to Worship Him (Matt. 2:1–8)**
   1. **Sincere seeking of the wise men (2:1, 2)**
   2. **Insincere seeking of Herod (2:3–8)**

II. **Wise Men's Search Rewarded (Matt. 2:9–11)**
   1. **Guided to joy (2:9, 10)**
   2. **Worshiping Jesus (2:11)**

III. **Herod's Search Thwarted (Matt. 2:12–23)**
   1. **The wise men's part in thwarting Herod (2:12)**
   2. **Divine deliverance of Jesus (2:13–23)**

The wise men sought the King of the Jews in order to worship Him (vv. 1, 2). Although Herod told the wise men that he intended to worship Jesus, he was lying (vv. 3–8). The wise men rejoiced when the star led them to the King (vv. 9, 10). They worshiped Jesus by bowing and offering Him treasures (v. 11). They obeyed God and left Judea without letting Herod know (v. 12). God delivered Jesus from the murderous intentions of Herod (vv. 13–23).

I. Seeking Jesus to Worship Him (Matt. 2:1–8)

1. Sincere seeking of the wise men (vv. 1, 2)

1 Now when Jesus was born in Bethlehem of Judaea in the days of Herod the king, behold, there came wise men from the east to Jerusalem,

2 Saying, Where is he that is born King of the Jews? for we have seen his star in the east, and are come to worship him.

The three main people in the drama of Matthew 2 are introduced in verse 1. Although Jesus was a child who played only a passive role in this drama, Jesus is the main person. God was actively at work throughout the drama to achieve His long-range purpose in His Son. Jesus is the King of the Jews whom the wise men sought and eventually found. He is the One whom Herod correctly saw as a threat to him, although not for the reasons he thought at the time. Although Jesus was the newborn

December 26 1999

King, He had no aspirations for Herod's paltry kind of reign or evil power.

The wise men play a key role in our annual retelling of the Christmas story; and although they appear only in Matthew 2:1–12, they played a key role in the biblical account of the coming of Jesus. Their role is somewhat like that of the shepherds in Luke 2. The first group to see the newborn King were the lowly shepherds. The wise men were probably the first to see the sign of His birth in the star; and although they did not arrive on the night of Jesus' birth, they were the first group in Matthew's account to worship Jesus.

The shepherds show that Christ came for the lowly, common people of the world. The wise men show that Jesus came for Gentiles, although high-born people, yet pagans by biblical standards. They were not kings, but a cross between astronomers and astrologers. Astronomy by our standards is a valid science of studying the universe. Astrology is an ancient superstition, consistently condemned in the Bible, that assumes our lives are governed by our astrological signs and predictions. Thus, by biblical standards, the wise men were pagan Gentiles.

Yet God used a star (of all things) to lead these pagan Gentiles to the Jewish King, who was destined also to be Savior of the world. They came from the east, probably Persia. When they spoke of seeing the star "in the east," they meant that they were to the east of Jerusalem when they saw it. They went to Jerusalem, which was the natural place to go in seeking a newborn King of the Jews. When they arrived, they announced to the current king of the Jews who they were, where they were from, and why they had come.

2. Insincere seeking of Herod (vv. 3–8)

> **3 When Herod the king had heard these things, he was troubled, and all Jerusalem with him.**

The words of the wise men shocked the city of Jerusalem. These foreigners did not know that Herod had spent much of his reign killing people whom he suspected of aspiring to be king of the Jews, and most of those Herod killed were members of his own family. However, the people of Jerusalem knew what Herod was like; and they were troubled because the coming of the wise men probably meant a new blood bath.

> **4 And when he had gathered all the chief priests and scribes of the people together, he demanded of them where Christ should be born.**
>
> **5 And they said unto him, In Bethlehem of Judaea: for thus it is written by the prophet,**
>
> **6 And thou Bethlehem, in the land of Juda, art not the least among the princes of Juda: for out of thee shall come a Governor, that shall rule my people Israel.**

Herod was only half-Jewish, and he was far from being a religious man; but he knew enough about Jewish religion to recognize "King of the Jews" as the title of the long-awaited Messiah of the Jews. Therefore, he called in the biblical scholars to tell him where the Messiah or Christ

December 26, 1999

was to be born. They quickly quoted to Herod the well-known prophecy of Micah 5:2, which named Bethlehem.

> **7 Then Herod, when he had privily called the wise men, enquired of them diligently what time the star appeared.**
>
> **8 And he sent them to Bethlehem, and said, Go and search diligently for the young child; and when ye have found him, bring me word again, that I may come and worship him also.**

Herod had a private meeting with the unsuspecting wise men. Herod was a wily man who knew how to use deceit to get what he wanted. He had found out where the Messiah was to be born. Then he pumped the wise men for information about when they first saw the star, thinking this would give him information needed to determine when the King was born. Since Herod later killed male babies under two years of age, two years represents the outer limits of what the wise men told Herod about when they saw the star.

Herod then told them to go to Bethlehem, a village only a few miles from Jerusalem. Herod apparently told them of Micah's prophecy. Using his polished skills at deception, Herod asked the wise men to send him word when they had found Jesus so that Herod could follow the wise men's example and worship the young child. Notice that Herod called Jesus "young child" (see also v. 11).

II. Wise Men's Search Rewarded (Matt. 2:9–11)

1. Guided to joy (vv. 9, 10)

> **9 When they had heard the king, they departed; and, lo, the star, which they saw in the east, went before them, till it came and stood over where the young child was.**
>
> **10 When they saw the star, they rejoiced with exceeding great joy.**

Some facts about the star are clear, but much remains a mystery. One fact is that the wise men saw the star while they were in the east, and they concluded that it heralded the birth of the King of the Jews (v. 2). Verses 9, 10 reveal these additional facts: The star led them as they left Jerusalem, it stopped over where Jesus was, and they felt great joy as a result. What is not clear is where the star was when they went to Jerusalem. Either the star had not been visible since they first saw it, or it had been stationary over Judea. At any rate, it now led them to the place in Bethlehem where Jesus was.

Their joy was not in the star, but in the One to whom it led them. When the star led them to where Jesus was, they knew that their long pilgrimage from the east was about to be rewarded.

2. Worshiping Jesus (v. 11)

> **11 And when they were come into the house, they saw the young child with Mary his mother, and fell down, and worshipped him: and when they had opened their treasures, they presented unto him gifts; gold, and frankincense, and myrrh.**

The words *house* and *young child* show that the wise men did not arrive on the night of Jesus' birth. Their worship of the King illustrates some of the marks of true worship: joy, reverence, and offerings. Worship is an act of veneration. These men fell down in reverence, awe, submission, and gratitude before the King.

Their offerings were called "treasures," which shows they were valuable. Gold is renowned for its value. Frankincense and myrrh were valuable spices and perfumes. The word *gifts* reminds us that offerings must be given voluntarily from among those things that God has blessed us with. (The Bible never tells us how many wise men came to worship Jesus. The number three probably was based on the assumption that each wise man brought an individual gift.)

III. Herod's Search Thwarted (Matt. 2:12–23)

1. The wise men's part in thwarting Herod (v. 12)

12 And being warned of God in a dream that they should not return to Herod, they departed into their own country another way.

The wise men apparently had been completely fooled by Herod. Therefore, they were probably about to send word to him as he had requested or perhaps even to stop in Jerusalem on their way home and tell him personally. However, God spoke to them in a dream and warned them about Herod. God told them not to let Herod know they had found Jesus.

These men were sensitive enough to God that they took this revelation as being from God. Therefore, they obeyed God's word and hid from Herod the information he had asked them to send him. Their act of faith and courage was the first part of God's plan to thwart the murderous intentions of Herod.

When the wise men left Bethlehem, they avoided going back the way they had come—through Jerusalem. If they had traveled through Jerusalem, Herod might have heard and had them apprehended. Even going another way was risky. Herod could have had someone following them. They were acting with courage in defying Herod's request. They were in danger as long as they were in lands ruled by Herod.

Matthew 2:12 is the last mention in the Bible of the wise men. Yet later—in the Book of Acts—we read how the good news was preached to all people. The wise men's coming to Jesus when He was only a young child foreshadowed the vast multitudes of non-Jews who would later come to Jesus as Savior of the world.

2. Divine deliverance of Jesus (vv. 13–23)

Joseph was a key human figure in God's deliverance of His Son. Joseph immediately obeyed the divine warning to flee Bethlehem by taking Jesus and Mary to Egypt (vv. 13–15). When Herod realized that he had been outwitted by the wise men, his murderous rage was vented by ordering the slaughter of Bethlehem's boys of two and under (vv. 16–18). After Joseph heard that Herod was dead, he also learned that Herod's evil son Archelaus reigned in Judea. A dream led him to go to Nazareth in Galilee (vv. 19–23).

Although God delivered Jesus as a young child from the murderous grasp of Herod, the Father allowed His Son later to place Himself in the

December 26, 1999

hands of those who wanted to kill Him. In this way, divine deliverance from sin and death was offered to all the lowly shepherds and pagan wise men of the world.

PRONUNCIATION GUIDE

Archelaus   [ahr kih LAY uhs]

SUMMARY OF BIBLE TRUTHS

1. Some seek Jesus sincerely in order to worship Him.
2. Some who claim to want to worship Jesus are insincere.
3. Those who sincerely seek Jesus find Him.
4. God often uses the most unlikely people to achieve His purpose.
5. Real worship includes joy; reverence; and generous, voluntary offerings.
6. God offers salvation to all people.

APPLYING THE BIBLE

1. What's a camel doing here? It could have happened in Bethlehem 2,000 years ago. But it happened in Maryland in 1998. On a cold, winter night, men dressed in the regal robes of wise men dragged the carcass of an Arabian camel off the highway.

The camel had been one of the star attractions in a live nativity scene. While his handlers were changing into their outfits, the camel broke free of his tether and ran for the highway.

Vinit Mody could not avoid the collision with the animal. He got out of the car and said, "What in the world is a camel doing on Route 50 in the United States of America? You only see a camel in the zoo."

One of the signs that we live in an increasingly secular society is that we no longer recognize the symbols of faith's most incredible story. More than a camel died on the highway that night. So did the sense of awe at what God did 2,000 years ago.

2. Worship defined. Seeing what God is worth, and then giving Him what He is worth.[1]

3. Worship anything you choose. "Satan doesn't care what we worship, so long as we don't worship God" (D. L. Moody).

4. Benefits of worship. The person who bows the lowest in the presence of God stands the straightest in the presence of sin.

5. Wise men and worship. Worship is the first step to wisdom.

6. We don't want to offend anyone. To avoid offending anybody, the schools dropped religion altogether and started singing about the weather. At my son's school, they now hold the winter program in February and sing increasingly nonmemorable songs such as "Winter Wonderland," "Frosty the Snowman," and—this is a real song—"Suzy Snowflake," all of which is pretty funny because we live in Miami. A visitor from another planet would assume that the children belonged to the Church of Meteorology.[2]

All this is a far cry from the reality of the anthem, "Joy to the world, the Lord is come, let earth receive her King!" And we are the poorer for it.

December 26, 1999

TEACHING THE BIBLE

- *Main Idea:* The wise men symbolize that Jesus came for Gentiles as well as Jews.
- *Suggested Teaching Aim:* To lead adults to list ways to worship Jesus sincerely.

A TEACHING OUTLINE

1. Seeking Jesus to Worship Him (Matt. 2:1–8)
2. Wise Men's Search Rewarded (Matt 2:9–11)
3. Herod's Search Thwarted (Matt. 2:12–13)

Introduce the Bible Study

Use number 1, "What's a Camel Doing Here?" in "Applying the Bible" to introduce the lesson.

Search for Biblical Truth

Organize the class into four groups. Ask each group to listen for one of the following:

- How the wise men followed God's will.
- How the wise men worshiped Jesus.
- How the wise men demonstrated great faith in the face of danger.
- How the wise men are examples for us.

Ask the groups to listen for ways the wise men accomplished their assigned function. Members will be asked to share their observations later. You might distribute paper and pencils.

IN ADVANCE, enlist two members to read aloud the Scripture. Ask them to read every other verse. Call for them to read Matthew 2:1–2 at this time. Ask members to share what they know about the wise men. **IN ADVANCE,** write the following chart on a large sheet of paper:

Compare and Contrast the Wise Men and the Shepherds

	Wise Men	Shepherds
Who were they?		
Where were they from?		
How did they learn of Jesus?		
How did they respond?		
How long did it take them to respond?		
How long did it take them to get to Jesus?		
Why do you think God revealed Jesus' birth to them?		

December 26, 1999

Ask the readers to read Matthew 2:3–8. Ask: Why was Jerusalem troubled when Herod heard about Jesus' birth? What approach did Herod take to the wise men's question? How did the chief priests and the scribes know where the Messiah was going to be born? (Locate Bethlehem and Jerusalem on a map showing Jesus' ministry.) What did Herod ask the wise men to do? What in Herod's response may indicate that the wise men came some time after Jesus' birth?

Ask the readers to read Matthew 2:9–10. Ask, What do we know about the star? (See "Studying the Bible.")

Before the reader reads Matthew 2:11, ask members to listen for marks of true worship in the wise men's adoration of Jesus and ask members to share their responses.

Ask the reader to read Matthew 2:12. Ask, What made the wise men's actions so dangerous?

Call for groups to share their responses to their assignments.

Give the Truth a Personal Focus

Read the six "Summary of Bible Truths" statements to summarize the lesson. Then read each statement again and ask members how that statement applies to their lives. Ask: What action do you need to take today to worship Jesus sincerely? Do you need to give Him a gift? Do you need to let Him use you to achieve His purpose? Do you need to accept His salvation? Challenge each member to respond in accordance with their individual needs.

---

1. Tim Keller, "What It Takes to Worship Well," *Leadership Journal,* Spring 1994, 19.
2. Dave Barry, "Notes on Western Civilization," *Chicago Tribune Magazine,* July 28, 1991.

The Disciples of Jesus

January 2, 2000

Background Passages: Matthew 4:18–22; 9:9–12; 10:1–4
Focal Passages: Matthew 4:18–22; 9:9–12; 10:1–4

In referring to "disciples" of Jesus, Matthew and the other New Testament writers sometimes meant a special group of twelve disciples and at times meant followers of Jesus other than the Twelve. The twelve disciples had a unique calling, relationship to Jesus, and mission; however, because they formed the nucleus of the church, we also learn from them some lessons about all disciples.

▶ **Study Aim:** *To name the unique characteristics of the twelve disciples and the basic lessons from them for all disciples.*

STUDYING THE BIBLE

OUTLINE AND SUMMARY
  I. Called to Follow Jesus (Matt. 4:18–22)
  II. Befriending Sinners in Jesus' Name (Matt. 9:9–12)
    1. Matthew the tax collector (9:9)
    2. Friend of sinners (9:10, 11)
    3. Physician for sinners (9:12)
  III. Sent Forth with Jesus' Authority (Matt. 10:1–4)

Jesus called four fishermen to follow Him and become fishers of men (4:18–22). Jesus called Matthew the tax collector (9:9). The Pharisees asked the disciples why Jesus ate with tax collectors and sinners (9:10, 11). Jesus compared Himself to a physician for people diseased by sin (9:12). Jesus sent the twelve apostles after giving them authority to heal and cast out evil spirits (10:1–4).

I. Called to Follow Jesus (Matt. 4:18–22)

18 And Jesus walking by the sea of Galilee, saw two brethren, Simon called Peter, and Andrew his brother, casting a net into the sea: for they were fishers.

19 And he saith unto them, Follow me, and I will make you fishers of men.

20 And they straightway left their nets, and followed him.

21 And going on from thence, he saw other two brethren, James the son of Zebedee, and John his brother, in a ship with Zebedee their father, mending their nets; and he called them.

22 And they immediately left the ship and their father, and followed him.

Early in Jesus' ministry in Galilee (Matt. 4:12–17), He called two pairs of brothers to be disciples. John 1:35–42 tells us of an earlier encounter with Andrew and Peter, and also probably with John. Matthew 4:18–22 describes how Jesus called Peter, Andrew, James, and John to full discipleship.

Although the word *disciples* is not used in Matthew 4:18–22, the call to "follow me" was a call to be disciples (Matt. 10:1). "Follow me" was an invitation of Jesus for people to commit themselves totally to Him, to learn from Him, to become like Him, and to be sent forth on mission for Him. Following Jesus in this way is what it means to be a disciple of His.

"Disciples" was a familiar term to describe pupils who attached themselves to a special teacher, often as live-in students. John the Baptist, for example, had disciples (Matt. 11:2). Thus, the Twelve were not the only followers of Jesus called "disciples." He had many other disciples during His public ministry (Matt. 8:21). The Book of Acts uses *disciples* as one of the terms to describe all who followed Jesus (Acts 11:26).

The Twelve were disciples in some special ways. They were chosen to be with Him during His incarnate ministry and later to tell of His teachings and be witnesses of His resurrection to all nations. Mark 3:13–17 says that Jesus called many to Himself, but He appointed twelve to be with Him, to be sent forth to preach, and to be given authority to heal the sick and cast out demons. Luke 6:12–16 calls these twelve "disciples" and "apostles."

In those days, a person ordinarily became a disciple by seeking out a teacher and joining his school. By contrast, Jesus took the initiative in seeking and calling His disciples. They did not choose Him; He chose them (John 15:16). This was true of the Twelve, and it is true of all His followers.

Jesus demands total commitment to Him. He said, "Follow me." Of course, people have a choice about whether to follow Him. In the case of the four fishermen, they immediately left everything and followed Jesus. People who were not willing to accept Jesus on His own terms could not become true disciples (Luke 9:57–62). In some cases, those called "disciples" proved false disciples by being unwilling to let Jesus fulfill His mission in His own way (John 6:66–69).

Jesus called the four fishermen to be "fishers of men." This showed that they were not just to be with Him and to learn from Him as pupils, but they were also to persuade others to become followers of Christ (see 10:1–4).

Parallelism is a characteristic of Hebrew poetry and of Hebrew thought in general. The Hebrews often emphasized something by repeating the same idea in slightly different words. In this case, the calls of James and John in verses 21, 22 have many parallels: two brothers, fishermen on the Sea of Galilee, called by Jesus, immediate obedience, left all, followed Jesus. By repeating these facts, Matthew emphasized the importance of being called as a disciple of Jesus.

II. Befriending Sinners in Jesus' Name (Matt. 9:9–12)
1. Matthew the tax collector (v. 9)

> 9 And as Jesus passed forth from thence, he saw a man, named Matthew, sitting at the receipt of custom: and he saith unto him, Follow me. And he arose, and followed him.

Matthew is sometimes called Levi (Mark 2:14). Like Simon Peter, Matthew Levi had two names. He collected customs fees, probably on goods passing along one of the roads near Capernaum. Tax collectors were hated by all the people because many of them used their positions of authority to demand more taxes than were due. They were hated by patriotic Jews because they collaborated with the Roman government, who controlled their lands. They were hated by pious groups like the Pharisees because the tax collectors became ceremonially unclean by associating with unclean people and things.

Significantly, Jesus chose as one of His disciples one of these hated "sinners." Matthew, like the four fishermen, was sought out and called by Jesus; and like them, he followed Jesus.

2. Friend of sinners (vv. 10, 11)

> **10 And it came to pass, as Jesus sat at meat in the house, behold, many publicans and sinners came and sat down with him and his disciples.**
>
> **11 And when the Pharisees saw it, they said unto his disciples, Why eateth your Master with publicans and sinners?**

Luke 5:29 indicates that Matthew Levi gave this feast and invited not only Jesus and His disciples but also some of his fellow tax collectors. The Pharisees were offended by this would-be rabbi eating with such people. The Pharisees defined just about everyone except Pharisees as "sinners" in the sense of not taking seriously the distinctions between clean and unclean things. However, among these "sinners" were some who were considered sinners even by Jesus (see, for example, Luke 7:37–48).

Jesus Himself often broke the Pharisees' rigid rules about what was unclean. Having table fellowship with unclean people was a flagrant abuse of their rules. To the Pharisees, one of Jesus' "sins" was that He was a friend of sinners (Luke 15:1, 2).

3. Physician for sinners (v. 12)

> **12 But when Jesus heard that, he said unto them, They that be whole need not a physician, but they that are sick.**

Jesus and the Pharisees had totally different strategies of evangelism. Because the Pharisees feared contamination, they avoided any close contact with sinners. They would accept repentant sinners if they came to the Pharisees, confessed their sins, and began to live by Pharisaic standards of righteousness. By contrast, Jesus sought out sinners, befriended them, and showed them God's love in order to lead them to repent (Luke 15:3–32; 19:10).

He illustrated this with the simple analogy of a physician going to the sick, not to healthy people. Jesus was not necessarily conceding that the Pharisees were truly righteous (see Matt. 5:20; Luke 18:9 14). He was simply accepting their basic premise that Jesus was eating with sinners. Jesus replied that since He had come to heal those who were diseased by sin, He obviously needed to spend time with those who were sick.

III. Sent Forth with Jesus' Authority (Matt. 10:1–4)

> **1 And when he had called unto him his twelve disciples, he gave them power against unclean spirits, to cast them out, and to heal all manner of sickness and all manner of disease.**
>
> **2 Now the names of the twelve apostles are these; The first, Simon, who is called Peter, and Andrew his brother; James the son of Zebedee, and John his brother;**

January 2, 2000

3 Philip, and Bartholomew; Thomas, and Matthew the publican; James the son of Alphaeus, and Lebbaeus, whose surname was Thaddaeus;

4 Simon the Canaanite, and Judas Iscariot, who also betrayed him.

Verse 1 assumes that Jesus called twelve disciples. Mark 3:13–19 and Luke 6:12–16 describe His appointment of the Twelve. Each of these passages lists the Twelve by name. Matthew lists the Twelve by name after describing how He gave them authority to perform miracles in His name. This authority was given as Jesus sent the Twelve out on a mission in His name. All the names in the three lists are not the same. This was because some of them were called by one of their two names. Bartholomew was probably the Nathanael of John 1:45–49. In Luke 6:16, Thaddaeus is called Judas, the brother of James, to distinguish him from Judas Iscariot. Because the Greek text says, Judas of James, some translators assume he was "the son of James" (NASB).

The mission, which is described in the rest of Matthew 10, is implied in Matthew's use of the word *apostles,* which means "those sent out." The mission of the twelve apostles is closely related to Matthew 9:36–38. Verse 36 describes Jesus' compassion for the multitudes, far more than He could personally help in His incarnate form. Thus, Jesus told the disciples that the harvest was far too great for the few harvesters; therefore, to pray that the Lord of the harvest would send forth workers. Matthew 10:5 says, "These twelve Jesus sent forth."

Their mission was primarily to preach (v. 7), but they were also given power or authority to perform miracles as signs of the kingdom whose coming they announced. Jesus Himself was engaged in a ministry of preaching, teaching, and healing (Matt. 4:23). Jesus performed miracles as acts of compassion (see Matt. 9:18–38, in the lesson for Jan. 16). Matthew 28:18–20 records the Great Commission, which Jesus gave to the apostles in a unique way, but which is given to all followers of Jesus in all ages. The emphasis in Matthew 28:18–20 is on Jesus giving His authority and commissioning His followers to make disciples of all nations by going, baptizing, and teaching.

The word *apostles* is occasionally used in the New Testament of missionaries in general, but the word normally was used to refer to this unique group of apostles. An apostle in the unique sense was someone who was a witness of the risen Lord and commissioned by the Lord as a bearer of His message to all the world. The New Testament is the inspired record of the unique testimony and teachings of these apostles. They have no successors; we have them with us as the Spirit of the risen Lord speaks to us through their writings in the New Testament.

PRONUNCIATION GUIDE

Alphaeus	[al FEE uhs]
Bartholomew	[bar THAHL uh myoo]
Capernaum	[kuh PURR nay uhm]
Lebbaeus	[luh BEE uhs]

Thaddaeus [THAD ih uhs]
Zebedee [ZEB uh dee]

SUMMARY OF BIBLE TRUTHS

1. Jesus called twelve disciples to follow Him with total commitment during His earthly ministry.
2. He sent them forth as apostles on a mission that foreshadowed their later mission to the whole world.
3. Although the twelve disciples were unique in some ways, in other ways they had characteristics of all true disciples.
4. Jesus seeks sinners and calls them to salvation and discipleship.
5. All disciples are to walk with the Lord, learn from Him, become like Him, and represent Him in the world.

APPLYING THE BIBLE

1. Cost of discipleship. "When Christ calls a man, he bids him come and die" (Dietrich Bonhoeffer).

2. The Twelve. It has been suggested that the twelve men selected by Jesus to be His disciples would not have made it in today's business environment. A response to Jesus from a business consulting firm in regard to the personality profiles of the Twelve might well have included Tim Hansel's imaginary assessment which reads in part:

"It is the staff opinion that most of your nominees are lacking in background, education and vocational aptitude for the type of enterprise you are undertaking. They do not have the team concept. We would recommend that you continue your search for persons of experience in managerial ability and proven capability.

"Simon Peter is emotionally unstable and given to fits of temper. Andrew has absolutely no qualities of leadership. The two brothers, James and John, the sons of Zebedee, place personal interest above company loyalty. Thomas demonstrates a questioning attitude that would tend to undermine morale. We feel that it is our duty to tell you that Matthew had been blacklisted by the Greater Jerusalem Better Business Bureau; James, the son of Alphaeus, and Thaddaeus definitely have radical leanings, and they both registered a high score on the manic-depressive scale.

"One of the candidates, however, shows great potential. He is a man of ability and resourcefulness, meets people well, has a keen business mind, and has contacts in high places. He is highly motivated, ambitious, and responsible. We recommend Judas Iscariot as your controller and right-hand man."[1]

3. Our friend. Jesus is called the friend of sinners. As His followers, we are supposed to love the things that Jesus loves. It is unthinkable that we would in turn reject the very ones that Christ would have spent His time with when He was on the earth in the flesh. We wear the letters WWJD (What Would Jesus Do?) on bracelets, but few of us have come to the point of abandoning ourselves to the ones Jesus went to.

4. Cost of a cross. Clarence Jordan, author of the "Cotton Patch" New Testament translation and founder of the interracial Koinonia Farm in Americus, Georgia, was getting a red-carpet tour of another minister's church. With pride the minister pointed to the rich, imported pews and luxurious decorations. As they stepped outside, darkness was falling, and a spotlight shone on a huge cross atop the steeple. "That cross alone cost us ten thousand dollars," the minister said with a satisfied smile.

"You got cheated," said Jordan. "Times were when Christians could get them for free."

5. Worth of discipleship. "A religion that gives nothing, costs nothing, and suffers nothing, is worth nothing" (Martin Luther).

6. The question. At the close of life, the question will not be:
- How much have you gotten? but How much have you given?
- How much have you won? but How much have you done?
- How much have you saved? but How much have you sacrificed?
- How much were you honored? but How much have you loved and served? (Nathan C. Schaeffer).

7. Tough training. "It is better to train ten people than to do the work of ten people. But it is harder" (D. L. Moody).

8. What mentors do. Leadership experts would use the term *mentoring* to describe what Jesus did. The following are things mentors do for those whom they mentor:
- set high expectations of performance,
- help build self confidence,
- encourage professional behavior,
- offer friendship,
- confront negative behaviors and attitudes,
- listen to personal problems,
- teach by example,
- provide growth experiences,
- explain how an organization works,
- coach mentorands,
- stand by mentorands in critical situations,
- offer wise counsel,
- inspire mentorands, and
- help with a mentorand's career.[2]

TEACHING THE BIBLE

- *Main Idea:* Jesus called people to follow and minister in His name.
- *Suggested Teaching Aim:* To lead adults to commit themselves to follow Jesus and minister in His name.

A TEACHING OUTLINE

1. *Called to Follow Jesus (Matt. 4:18–22)*
2. *Befriending Sinners in Jesus' Name (Matt. 9:9–12)*
3. *Sent Forth on Mission (Matt. 10:1–4)*

Introduce the Bible Study

Ask, If you had been Jesus, what kind of disciples would you have called? Use number 2, "The Twelve," in "Applying the Bible" to introduce the lesson.

Search for Biblical Truth

Ask members to open their Bibles to Matthew 4:18–22. Write on a chalkboard or a large sheet of paper: *Disciple* and *Apostle*. Ask: What is the difference between a disciple and an apostle? (Basically, there is little difference in the way the New Testament refers to the two; a disciple is a "follower" and an apostle is "one who is sent out.")

Ask if anyone can name all twelve of Jesus' apostles. Ask: Who was the first disciple Jesus called? What did Jesus ask the men He called to do? ("Commit themselves totally to Him, to learn from Him, to become like Him, and to be sent forth on mission for Him.") Ask, Would you agree with this statement from "Applying the Bible": "When Jesus calls a man, He bids him come and die"?

DISCUSS: Does Jesus call followers at a lesser level of commitment today than He did in the first century? Why do you think so? What does that imply about our discipleship?

Ask a volunteer to read Matthew 9:9–11 aloud. Ask, Why would Jesus call a man whose title of office was used as a synonym for a cheat, who was hated by the patriotic Jews for collaborating with Rome, and who was hated by the religious groups because he was ceremonially unclean?

Ask someone to read Luke 5:29. What was one of Matthew's first actions after accepting Jesus' call? Why do you think Matthew did this? Why did the religious leaders object?

DISCUSS: How can we reach out to people who will not come inside a church building?

Ask a volunteer to read aloud Matthew 10:1–4. Ask, Are any of the names of the Twelve unfamiliar to you? Why? (Many likely had two names, like Simon Peter, and one list would list one name and another would list another name.)

Give the Truth a Personal Focus

Explain: Today the term *mentoring* has become quite popular. It means to guide, coach, train, instruct, tutor. A person becomes a mentor to someone else. Read number 8, "What Mentors Do," in "Applying the Bible." Ask: How good a job does our church do in mentoring new Christians? How can we improve?

Lead in prayer that the members will commit themselves to follow Jesus and minister in His name.

---

1. Tim Hansel, *Eating Problems for Breakfast* (Word Publishing, 1988), 194-195.
2. Clinton and Clinton, *The Mentor Handbook* (Altadena, Calif.: Barnabas Publishers, 1991), from the Preface.

January 9, 2000

Teachings on Prayer

Background Passage: Matthew 6:1–15
Focal Passage: Matthew 6:1–15

Matthew's Gospel gives special attention to the teachings of Jesus. For example, it contains the Sermon on the Mount (Matt. 5–7). Within that sermon is a section on right motives for religious duties: giving, praying, and fasting. Attached to the verses about right motives about praying are some other teachings about prayer.

♦**Study Aim:** *To distinguish what Jesus taught about how not to pray from what He taught about how to pray.*

STUDYING THE BIBLE

OUTLINE AND SUMMARY
I. How Not to Pray (Matt. 6:1–8)
   1. Don't pray to get people's attention (6:1–6)
   2. Don't pray to get God's attention (6:7, 8)
II. How to Pray (Matt. 6:9–15)
   1. Praise God (6:9, 10)
   2. Ask God for what you need (6:11–13)
   3. Live as you pray (6:14, 15)

Don't pray in such a way as to seek human attention and praise (vv. 1–6). Don't pray as if prayers are necessary to inform God or get Him to care (vv. 7, 8). Praise God our Father and ask Him to glorify His name, complete His work, accomplish His will (vv. 9, 10). Ask God for daily bread, forgiveness, and deliverance from temptation (vv. 11–13). Live as we pray by forgiving others as God has forgiven us (vv. 14, 15).

I. How Not to Pray (Matt. 6:1–8)
1. Don't pray to get people's attention (vv. 1–6)

> 1 Take heed that ye do not your alms before men, to be seen of them: otherwise ye have no reward of your Father which is in heaven.
>
> 2 Therefore when thou doest thine alms, do not sound a trumpet before thee, as the hypocrites do in the synagogues and in the streets, that they may have glory of men. Verily I say unto you, They have their reward.
>
> 3 But when thou doest alms, let not thy left hand know what thy right hand doeth:
>
> 4 That thine alms may be in secret: and thy Father which seeth in secret himself shall reward thee openly.

The word *alms* in verse 1 is "righteousness" in many ancient copies of Matthew. This is an introductory verse to three examples of religious duties: giving (vv. 2–4), praying (vv. 5, 6), and fasting (vv. 16–18). In between verses 6 and 16 are further teachings about prayer. The point in verse 1 is not that people of faith ought not perform religious duties. The warning is against doing religious duties for the wrong reason: in order to get people's attention and thus their praise.

Giving to the needy is a duty for all people of faith, but giving is not to be done in order to draw attention to the person who is giving. Hypocritical people make a big flourish about their giving in order to win the praise of others. Jesus said that such human praise is the only reward these seekers of human praise will receive.

Verse 3 puzzles many people. Jesus was not saying that we should not be aware of what we give. His point was that we should not take personal pride in our gifts.

5 And when thou prayest, thou shalt not be as the hypocrites are: for they love to pray standing in the synagogues and in the corners of the streets, that they may be seen of men. Verily I say unto you, They have their reward.

6 But thou, when thou prayest, enter into thy closet, and when thou hast shut thy door, pray to thy Father which is in secret; and thy Father which seeth in secret shall reward thee openly.

Jesus was not forbidding praying in public. He was warning against praying in order to be seen and praised by others. If that is our reason for praying, the praise we get will be our only reward. The Bible gives examples of people leading in public praying and of individuals praying in ways that were visible to others, but sincere people of prayer don't pray in order to get the attention and thus win the praise of others.

The foundation for our praying is a time of private communion with God. The description of a specific place implies that such a personal prayer time ought to be part of our daily lives.

2. Don't pray to get God's attention (vv. 7, 8)

7 But when ye pray, use not vain repetitions, as the heathen do: for they think that they shall be heard for their much speaking.

8 Be not ye therefore like unto them: for your Father knoweth what things ye have need of, before ye ask him.

Heathen prayers assume that the gods either don't know or don't care about human needs and can be moved to act when people repeat certain prayer words. Jesus taught that such praying is heathen because it denies trust in the heavenly Father. We do not need to pray in order to inform God of our needs or to convince Him to care enough to do something about our needs. He already knows and cares.

"Much speaking" does not forbid long prayers. The Bible contains some long prayers. For example, Solomon's prayer of dedication for the temple was long (2 Chron. 6).

"Repetitions" does not forbid persistent praying. Jesus taught persistence in praying. Some of Jesus' parables emphasized that true needs are always expressed over and over (Luke 11:5–8; 18:1–8). A superficial reading of these parables might seem to imply that God is reluctant to heed our prayers and must be persuaded by constant praying on our part. However, Jesus' point is that true prayer, by its very nature, is persistent.

January 9, 2000

The references to God as Father in Matthew 7:9–11; Luke 11:9–13 reinforce the reference to God as our Father in Matthew 6:8.

Someone may ask, "If God already knows and cares, why do we need to pray at all?" Here are four reasons:

- Many of our greatest needs can only be met when we recognize them and ask God for them. God wants to save all people, but He has made salvation conditioned on our prayers of confession and trust.
- Our greatest ongoing need is communion with God, and prayer is primarily communion with God.
- God has ordained that He uses human prayers to work out His will in the world.
- When we pray, we ourselves are transformed.

II. How to Pray (Matt. 6:9–15)

1. Praise God (vv. 9, 10)

> **9 After this manner therefore pray ye: Our Father which art in heaven, Hallowed be thy name.**
>
> **10 Thy kingdom come. Thy will be done in earth, as it is in heaven.**

Instead of the proud praying of the hypocrites or the vain babblings of the heathen, how should one pray to the Father who already knows and cares? Jesus answered that question by giving the Model Prayer, usually called the Lord's Prayer.

When we say "our Father," we show that we are part of the family of faith that praises and prays to the same Father. The famous Psalm 23 begins, "The LORD is my Shepherd." God is our Father and my Father. He must be real to each of us; however, we realize that He is near to all who know Him. When we add "which art in heaven," we are acknowledging His infinite greatness and His intimate closeness.

The Model Prayer begins with three petitions in a spirit of praise to our heavenly Father. We pray that His name be glorified, that His kingdom come in all its fullness, and that His will be done on earth as in heaven. Notice that these are not prayers that we be able to glorify Him, bring in His kingdom, and do His will. These are all appropriate prayers; but this prayer is addressed to the only One who can bring these things to pass—whether through human instruments or in some other way.

2. Ask God for what you need (vv. 11–13)

> **11 Give us this day our daily bread.**
>
> **12 And forgive us our debts, as we forgive our debtors.**
>
> **13 And lead us not into temptation, but deliver us from evil: For thine is the kingdom, and the power, and the glory, for ever. Amen.**

The second group of three petitions focuses on our own needs. Everyone needs bread. In commenting on Jesus' quotation of Deuteronomy 8:3 in Matthew 4:4, we noted that we do not live by bread alone but we do need bread to live physically. When Jesus ate, He said a prayer (Matt. 14:19). So should we. Because we are dependent on God for all our needs, we express our thanks for bread in the past and our dependence on God for future bread. We do this daily. The trust in this prayer is similar to the trust Jesus advocated as an antidote for anxiety (Matt. 6:25–34).

All of us need forgiveness, even people who have trusted Jesus as Savior (1 John 1:9, 10). Unconfessed sin is unforsaken sin, and it stands as a barrier to our joy in the Lord and our usefulness in His kingdom.

Not only do we sin against God, but also sin against one another. Jesus taught us to seek reconciliation whether the sin is ours (Matt. 5:23, 24) or another's against us (Matt. 18:15–20). Thus, whenever we pray to the Father for His forgiveness, we affirm that we have forgiven those who have sinned against us. As we shall see in verses 14, 15, these two are inseparable.

The third petition has two parts. "Lead us not into evil" may imply that God is the author of temptations to do evil. When we studied the temptations, we noted Matthew 4:1, "Then was Jesus led up of the spirit into the wilderness to be tempted of the devil." In commenting on that verse, we distinguished between two meanings of the same Greek word: test and tempt. The Bible denies that God ever tempts anyone to do evil (James 1:13–15). However, God does allow us to be tested in order to mature in our faith and endurance. The devil, however, seeks to turn each situation in which we are tested into a temptation to do evil.

Thus, the first part of verse 13 may be a request that God honor His promise not to allow us to face tests beyond our capacity to endure (1 Cor. 10:13). We know we are weak, and thus we ask the Father not to subject us to great tests.

Some Bible students think that both parts of the verse express the same prayer in different words. In other words, "lead us not into temptation" is another way of saying, "deliver us from evil." This would be consistent with Hebrew parallelism, in which the same idea is repeated in slightly different words. If so, "lead us not into temptation" means "don't let us fall prey to temptation."

The word *evil* can mean "evil thing" or "evil one." Many translators think Jesus had in mind a prayer to be able to overcome the temptations of the devil. The Bible assumes this can be done, but only as we meet Satan in the power of God (James 4:7; 1 Cor. 10:13; Eph. 6:10–18).

3. Live as you pray (vv. 14, 15)

14 For if ye forgive men their trespasses, your heavenly Father will also forgive you:

15 But if ye forgive not men their trespasses, neither will your Father forgive your trespasses.

Our lives must be consistent with our prayers. One example of this principle is seen in verses 14 and 15. These verses emphasize that the two kinds of forgiveness in verse 12 are inseparable. Jesus elaborated on this in the parable of the unforgiving servant, which He told after Peter asked about how often to forgive someone (Matt. 18:21–35). Be careful not to misunderstand what Jesus was teaching. He was not teaching that forgiving others is a good work that merits God forgiving our sins.

His point is that forgiveness is not a one-way street, in which the only direction for forgiveness is from God into our hearts and lives. Forgiveness is like a two-way street in which traffic flows in both directions: from God to us and from us to others. The person who closes His heart in either direction closes it in the other. The person whose heart is open to receive God's forgiveness is also a person who freely offers forgiveness to others. A heart that is closed to forgiveness flowing out is closed to forgiveness flowing in.

SUMMARY OF BIBLE TRUTHS

1. Don't pray in order to be seen and praised by others.
2. Don't pray as if God does not know and care about us.
3. Praise the heavenly Father and ask Him to glorify His name, bring in His kingdom, and accomplish His sovereign will.
4. Ask God for daily bread, forgiveness, and deliverance from evil.
5. The heart that is open to receive God's forgiveness is also open for forgiveness to flow out to others.

APPLYING THE BIBLE

1. The greater work. "Prayer does not fit us for the greater works; prayer is the greater work" (Oswald Chambers).

2. Three facets of prayer. While lecturing on the Sermon on the Mount, David Perkins, New Testament professor, New Orleans Baptist Seminary, said forgiveness is like a three-faceted diamond. First, forgiveness is causative. Because we have been forgiven, we must forgive others. Second, forgiveness is comparative. We are asking God to forgive us just as we forgive others. Third, forgiveness is resultative. If we expect God to forgive us, we must not stop forgiving others.

3. God's go-ahead. Pastor Bill Hybels has an insight on prayer that is easy to remember:
- When I am wrong, God says "grow."
- When the timing is wrong, God says "slow."
- When the request is wrong, God says "no."
- But when I am right, the timing is right, and the request is right, God says "go."[1]

4. Friendship with God. Roberta C. Bondi, author and teacher, says intercessory prayer is based upon our friendship with God. This doesn't mean that God wants what we want, but that we want what God wants. If God's deepest longing is for the well-being of the world, then God wants the well-being of war-torn countries, the homeless, the sick and diseased. We intercede in prayer for these things out of friendship with God.[2]

5. Three elements of prayer. Roberta C. Bondi suggests steps for the individual having difficulty "learning to pray," encouraging them to include three elements in their prayer. (1) Read a favorite Scripture passage as a part of your prayer. The Psalms and many of Paul's letters contain wonderful prayers. (2) Remember that prayer is simply conversation with God in which you really speak your mind. (3) Learn to listen, be silent in God's presence without saying anything.[3]

6. Driven to pray. Jean-Paul Kaufmann, a French journalist, was freed by Muslim terrorists in 1988 after three years in captivity. In an interview, he gave this chilling account.

"It was the second or third day, and I was sitting tied to a chair in a dark room. I felt in that solitude that I had no one to speak to but God. I felt very close to Him then, perhaps because there was no one to distract me. I feel further removed from God now that I am back with my family in comfortable surroundings. In that prison, I was face-to-face with God. I almost miss the luxury of that solitude. I have nostalgia for that intimacy with God. I try to find it now in my house in the country, but the intensity cannot be repeated.

"I knew that God was with me in my ordeal. I can't tell you how I knew, I just did. I felt that He would protect me. I avoided the opportunistic trade of favors: I'll do this for you if you do that for me. I just said to Him, 'Let Your will be done.'"

7. Unusual forms of prayer. Laurence A. Wagley, professor of preaching and worship at Saint Paul School of Theology (United Methodist), in Kansas City, Missouri, characterizes prayer in unusual ways.

- **Listening as prayer.** Listening to music, to the wind in the trees, to the noise of the city may be a form of prayer. "Be still and know that I am God."
- **Prayer as remembering.** The central act of the holiest prayer—the eucharistic prayer—is remembering.
- **Prayer when you can't think of anything else.** This is the prayer of crisis, of panic and trouble. "O God, get me out of this!" Children pray, "God, don't let it happen," or "Don't let it have happened."
- **Prayer to go to sleep by.** This would be characterized by a quiet sense of well-being.
- **Prayer during wasted time or during underutilized time.** Prayer while driving, vacuuming, mowing the lawn, waiting—this is a natural turning to God in which we discover that God has been close all the time.
- **Non-discursive prayer.** Practicing the presence of God without words.

TEACHING THE BIBLE

- *Main Idea:* Jesus taught His disciples how to pray.
- *Suggested Teaching Aim:* To lead adults to identify characteristics of prayer Jesus taught.

A TEACHING OUTLINE

1. *How Not to Pray (Matt. 6:1–8)*
2. *How to Pray (Matt. 6:9–15)*

January 9, 2000

Introduce the Bible Study
Use number 5, "Three Elements of Prayer," in "Applying the Bible" to introduce the lesson.

Search for Biblical Truth
◆ Write the following on a chalkboard or a large sheet of paper:

When You Pray	
Don't:	Do:

Ask members to open their Bibles to Matthew 6:1–8 and read these verses silently to find Jesus' teachings on how *not* to pray. List these under *Don't*. Ask members to read different translations of verse 3 to clarify what Jesus was *not* saying. Ask, How can we know that in verse 6 Jesus was not forbidding us to pray in public?

Ask members to read silently Matthew 6:7–8. Using the material in "Studying the Bible," explain Jesus' objection to "much speaking" and "vain repetitions."

IN ADVANCE, on four small strips of paper, copy the four reasons why we need to pray if God already knows and cares. Distribute these to four different people and ask them to read the statement and comment on it.

Ask members to add additional *Don'ts* to the list.

Ask members to read silently Matthew 6:9–15 to find how Jesus said we should pray. List these under *Do* on the chart.

Organize members into three groups and give each group one of the following sets of questions. Allow about five minutes for study and then call for responses. (Use these questions with the entire group if your members do not respond well to groups.)

1. Praise God (Matt. 6:9–10)
Based on the above verses:
◆ What does praying "Our Father" indicate about our relationship with other believers and God's intimate closeness?
◆ What does "in heaven" indicate about God's infinite greatness?

2. Ask God for What You Need (Matt. 6:11–13)
Based on the above verses:
◆ What does the request for physical bread indicate about the relationship of the physical and spiritual?
◆ What happens if believers do not confess their sins?
◆ Why does God allow us to be tested?
◆ How can we overcome the temptations of the devil?

3. Live as You Pray (Matt. 6:14–15)
Based on the above verses:
◆ What is the relationship between forgiving others and receiving forgiveness?
◆ Why is forgiving others not a good work that merits God's forgiveness of our sins?

- Can a person who has experienced God's wonderful forgiveness of sin harbor an unforgiving spirit toward another person?

Ask members if they can add any additional *Do's* to the list.

Give the Truth a Personal Focus

Distribute paper and pencils. Ask them to look at the list of *Do's* and *Don'ts* and select one statement from each list that they will covenant to work on this week. Close by sharing illustration No. 6, "Driven to Pray," in "Applying the Bible."

---

1. Bill Hybels, *Too Busy Not to Pray*.
2. "Learning to Pray: An Interview with Roberta C. Bondi," *The Christian Century*, March 20, 1996, 326.
3. Ibid.

January 16 2000

Miracles of Compassion

Background Passage: Matthew 9:18–38
Focal Passages: Matthew 9:18–31, 35, 36

Miracles were a prominent feature of Jesus' ministry. Many were acts of compassion designed to help desperate people. Many of these people were not treated with compassion by anyone but Jesus. Because Jesus saw all life as valuable, He acted with compassion toward the dying and their families, toward the chronically ill, toward the unclean, and toward people with disabilities.

▶**Study Aim:** *To resolve to act with compassion that affirms the value of all people and human life.*

STUDYING THE BIBLE

OUTLINE AND SUMMARY
  I. **Miracles That Helped Desperate People (Matt. 9:18–34)**
     1. **A distraught father (9:18, 19)**
     2. **A seriously ill woman 9:20–22)**
     3. **Grieving parents (9:23–26)**
     4. **Two blind men (9:27–31)**
     5. **A demoniac who could not speak (9:32–34)**
  II. **Ministry of Compassion (Matt. 9:35–38)**

When a distraught father asked Jesus to come because his daughter was all but dead, Jesus followed him (vv. 18, 19). Jesus healed a seriously ill woman who showed her faith by touching His clothes (vv. 20–22). Jesus called a dead girl back to life (vv. 23–26). He opened the eyes of two blind men in response to their bold faith (vv. 27–31). When Jesus cast a demon out of a man, the man was able to speak (vv. 32–34). Jesus' ministry was motivated by His compassion for people, whom He saw as shepherdless sheep and as a vast harvest field with few harvesters (vv. 35–38).

I. Miracles That Helped Desperate People (Matt. 9:18–34)

1. A distraught father (vv. 18, 19)

> 18 While he spake these things unto them, behold, there came a certain ruler, and worshipped him, saying, My daughter is even now dead: but come and lay thy hand upon her, and she shall live.
>
> 19 And Jesus arose, and followed him, and so did his disciples.

You may want to read Mark 5:21–43 and Luke 8:40–56, the longer accounts of the two miracles of Matthew 9:18–26. From them, we learn that the name of the ruler was Jairus, and that he was a ruler of the syn-

January 16 2000

agogue. Only Matthew, however, tells us that the ruler worshiped Jesus as he made his request.

The exact time of the daughter's death is not clear. Our translation of Matthew 9:18 has the ruler tell Jesus, "My daughter is even now dead." But "is even now dead" could be translated "has just come to the point of death." This is similar to "lieth at the point of death" in Mark 5:23. The ruler felt that she was dead or as good as dead. He thus showed great faith in asking Jesus to help someone caught in the clutches of death.

Notice that Matthew uses the word "followed" to describe Jesus' response. This is the same word that Jesus used to call people to become His disciples. Now in response to the desperation and faith of this father, "Jesus arose, and followed him."

2. A seriously ill woman (vv. 20–22)

> 20 And, behold, a woman, which was diseased with an issue of blood twelve years, came behind him, and touched the hem of his garment:
>
> 21 For she said within herself, If I may but touch his garment, I shall be whole.
>
> 22 But Jesus turned him about, and when he saw her, he said, Daughter, be of good comfort; thy faith hath made thee whole. And the woman was made whole from that hour.

Matthew tells us that the woman had been losing blood for twelve years. Mark 5:26 adds, she "had suffered many things of many physicians, and had spent all that she had, and was nothing bettered, but rather grew worse." We also know from Leviticus 15:25–27 that her condition made her ceremonially unclean.

When she heard that Jesus was near, she joined the crowd following Him. She was reluctant to get in front of Him and make her request. Therefore, she came up with the plan to touch His garment, hoping that the touch might heal her. The form of her words in verse 21 had more uncertainty than the translation reveals. Yet even so, hers was amazing faith to dare to hope that merely touching His clothes could heal her.

Mark 5:30–34 elaborates on what happened when she touched the hem of His garment. He asked who had touched Him. Jesus had felt power flow from Him. The frightened woman confessed that she had touched Him. Matthew and Mark both tell how Jesus calmed the woman's fears and assured her that her faith had healed her. The healing coincided with the time of her touch of faith.

3. Grieving parents (vv. 23–26)

> 23 And when Jesus came into the ruler's house, and saw the minstrels and the people making a noise,
>
> 24 He said unto them, Give place: for the maid is not dead, but sleepeth. And they laughed him to scorn.
>
> 25 But when the people were put forth, he went in, and took her by the hand, and the maid arose.
>
> 26 And the fame hereof went abroad into all that land.

Many of Jesus' most important opportunities to help people might have appeared to others to be interruptions. Matthew 9:18 has the ruler

January 16, 2000

coming to Jesus while He was teaching. The woman had interrupted Jesus on His urgent mission to the ruler's house. We can only imagine how Jairus was feeling during this delay in getting to the bedside of his little girl.

As Jesus approached the house, He heard the familiar sounds of a first-century Jewish mourning for the dead. The custom was for the bereaved family to hire flute players, who played sad music, and mourners, who wailed loudly. Even a poor family was expected to hire at least two flute players and one woman wailer. As a prominent person, Jairus probably had more than one professional mourner.

All this sounded like "noise" to Jesus. "Give place" means "leave" or "get out." He told the professional mourners to leave because He claimed the dead girl was not dead, but sleeping. What happened next showed the superficiality of the pretended mourning. They laughed at Jesus and His words. His response was to force them to leave. This is the meaning of the rather mild translation "the people were put forth."

Then Jesus went in and brought the dead child back to life. This was His intended meaning of the words "not dead, but sleepeth." Jesus was not denying that she was really dead, for she was. Neither was He implying anything about the state of the dead as some kind of suspended animation or soul sleep. He was saying that from God's point of view, the condition of the dead is not hopeless and lifeless. The person who is literally asleep will wake up. Jesus was saying that in the same way, He had the power to overcome death and cause the dead to live.

The Gospels give three examples of Jesus recalling dead people to life: Jairus's daughter, the only son of the widow of Nain (Luke 7:11–17), and Lazarus (John 11:1–44). Each of these miracles was a restoration to physical life. These victories over death foreshadowed the unique resurrection of Jesus Himself. Jesus was not just restored to physical life, later to die. He conquered death once and for all. He has dominion over death and is alive forever. And because He lives, those who know Him as Lord and Savior will live also.

4. Two blind men (vv. 27–31)

> **27** And when Jesus departed thence, two blind men followed him, crying, and saying, Thou Son of David, have mercy on us.
>
> **28** And when he was come into the house, the blind men came to him: and Jesus saith unto them, Believe ye that I am able to do this? They said unto him, Yea, Lord.
>
> **29** Then touched he their eyes, saying, According to your faith be it unto you.
>
> **30** And their eyes were opened; and Jesus straitly charged them, saying, See that no man know it.
>
> **31** But they, when they were departed, spread abroad his fame in all that country.

The distraught ruler, his grieving wife, and the seriously ill woman were all in desperate conditions. So were these two blind men. Like the ruler and the woman, these two came to Jesus. As they groped along following Jesus, they cried out loudly for all to hear as they asked Jesus to show mercy on them.

Jesus acted as if He had not heard them. He continued on His way and entered the house. The blind men were made bold by their desperate plight and by their faith. We wonder why Jesus did not stop as soon as they cried out. We cannot fathom the ways of the Lord, but His words to them give two strong clues to His reasons.

1. He asked them if they really believed. Thus, His failure to respond immediately seems to have tested the reality of their faith. After they both assured Jesus, whom they called "Lord," that they truly believed, Jesus touched their eyes. "According to your faith" means "in response to your faith." His healing touch and authoritative word opened the eyes of these two blind men.

2. The other reason for His reluctance is seen in His strong command to the two men not to tell others what had happened. Such commands were common during Jesus' public ministry. These puzzle many people in light of the commands after His resurrection to tell everyone. The most likely explanation for Jesus telling people not to spread the word about His miracles was the distorted expectation of many first-century Jews concerning the Messiah. Many were looking for an earthly king, who would use divine power to establish Himself and restore Israel to its lost glory.

These two men had called Jesus "Son of David," a favorite title for the Messiah and one that often expected the "Son of David" to restore the glory of Israel under David. Jesus did not want to become known primarily as a worker of miracles because it would feed that false expectation. This false expectation made it all the more difficult for Jesus to fulfill His real role as King and Suffering Servant.

5. A demoniac who could not speak (vv. 32–34)

When Jesus cast a demon out of a man who could not speak, the man was able to speak (vv. 32, 33a). The people were amazed, but the Pharisees accused Jesus of performing this miracle with Satan's help (vv. 33b, 34).

II. Ministry of Compassion (Matt. 9:35–38)

35 And Jesus went about all the cities and villages, teaching in their synagogues, and preaching the gospel of the kingdom, and healing every sickness and every disease among the people.

36 But when he saw the multitudes, he was moved with compassion on them, because they fainted, and were scattered abroad, as sheep having no shepherd.

Matthew 9:35 repeats Matthew 4:23. In between are examples of each of three aspects of Jesus' ministry, especially His teachings and His miracles.

Verse 36 is a transition verse. It sums up the motive for what Jesus had done and what He was about to do. "Compassion" means to be so deeply moved with concern for others that one takes action to help. Jesus looked at the crowds and was moved with compassion because they were like sheep without a shepherd. "Fainted" means "harassed," and

January 16, 2000

"scattered abroad" means "helpless." Jesus was concerned because He was the Shepherd from whom they had strayed.

Jesus also compared the spiritual needs of people to a vast harvest field. He challenged the Twelve to pray that the Lord of the harvest would send forth workers into the field (vv. 37, 38).

First-century Gentiles placed little value on human life. Abortion and child exposure, for example, were common. Even Jews often ignored people who were chronically ill, who had disabilities, or who were considered unclean. They offered little real hope for the dying and for the bereaved. By contrast, Jesus, who was moved with compassion toward all people, acted to give love, hope, and help to all. Thus, this is an appropriate lesson for Sanctity of Human Life Sunday.

PRONUNCIATION GUIDE

Jairus [JIGH ruhs]
Lazarus [LAZ uh ruhs]

SUMMARY OF BIBLE TRUTHS

1. Affirm the value of all human life by acts of compassion.
2. Help the helpless and hopeless.
3. Show compassion on the dying and their families.
4. Help the bereaved find hope.
5. Take time for the chronically ill.
6. Treat people who have disabilities with respect and love.

APPLYING THE BIBLE

1. The power of compassion. When you think about compassion, you generally think of people who give themselves away to others like obscure missionaries, teachers committed to the inner cities, and relief workers who labor for little in return. No one usually thinks about rock and roll stars. Yet in 1984 at the height of the Ethiopian famine, a British rocker named Bob Geldof was moved to raise nearly 72,000 British pounds ($100,000 in U.S. currency) after watching the evening news. He did this in only a very few months and in the process motivated American musicians to sponsor a similar event. Millions of dollars became available to feed hungry people a world away all because somebody did something.

What motivated Bob Geldof was compassion. He saw a need, and he did what he could to meet it. If today's church would only demonstrate half of the compassion for the lost and hurting of our world as Geldof did, our world would be in much better shape.

2. Funeral customs. Tennessee Williams wrote, "Funerals are pretty compared with death."[1] He may well have considered the funeral customs of Jesus' day. A little girl lay dead, and while nothing was pretty about that, custom demanded that professional mourners be hired. The shallowness of the funeral demonstrates the compassion of Jesus. He saw the meaningless rut we were in and came to change it.

January 16 2000

3. Evidence of compassion. One day a student asked anthropologist Margaret Mead for the earliest sign of civilization in a given culture. He expected the answer to be a clay pot or perhaps a fish hook or grinding stone. Her answer was, "A healed femur." Mead explained that no healed femurs are found where the law of the jungle, survival of the fittest, reigns. A healed femur shows that someone cared. Someone had to do that injured person's hunting and gathering until the leg healed. The evidence of compassion is the first sign of civilization.[2]

4. How to cultivate compassion:
- Practice kindness and grace while driving in rush hour this week.
- Become a volunteer in a homeless shelter for one night during the holidays this year.
- Do something compassionate for a family who is watching a loved one die.
- Write a "thinking of you" card on the death anniversary to encourage a widow.
- Adopt a nursing home resident and visit this person once a month for the coming year.
- Start looking for people with disabilities and become a servant to them in some small way.

5. Setting an example:
- Be responsive to the needs of your child. Feeling cared for makes a child feel secure and connected to other people, so that he or she, in turn, can care for others.
- Encourage your child to be helpful to others. When a child helps out and realizes how good she has made others feel, she will feel satisfied and will begin to see herself as a helpful person.
- When your child begins to say or do something mean, explain how these behaviors make others feel, and gently remind him of a time when someone hurt him.
- Make a habit of extending common courtesy and respect to others, strangers included. For instance, let a driver who needs to turn onto the main road pull in front of you, or help an elderly person manage her cart at the supermarket. Let your children see you taking time for others in a non-resentful way.
- Demonstrate a strong sense of honesty. Don't say, "Tell her I'm not here," when the phone is for you.
- Praise good and kind behavior . . . and praise it again.[3]

6. Compassion fatigue. For those who feel they have given too much, there is a trendy new ailment that has been diagnosed. Just when we thought there were no more excuses, someone has coined the phrase "compassion fatigue." Anna Quindlen says, "People sometimes suffer from compassion fatigue when they are overwhelmed at the needs and hurts of people, such as competing tragedies, breast cancer, heart disease, homelessness, hunger, famine, domestic crime, teenage pregnancy, rape, and addicted babies. Compassion fatigue is the result of not know-

January 16, 2000

ing who to help first."[4] The danger of compassion fatigue is that soon, overwhelmed by it all, no one will be helped at all.

TEACHING THE BIBLE

▸ *Main Idea:* Jesus' compassion affirmed the value of all people and human life.

▸ *Suggested Teaching Aim:* To lead adults to identify persons to whom they can show compassion.

A TEACHING OUTLINE

1. Miracles that Helped Desperate People (Matt. 9:18–34)
2. Ministry of Compassion (Matt. 9:35–38)

Introduce the Bible Study

Use number 3, "Evidence of Compassion," in "Applying the Bible" to introduce the lesson.

Search for Biblical Truth

IN ADVANCE, on separate strips of paper write each of the following:

How do you think . . .

. . . Jairus felt when he came to Jesus? (1)
. . . Jesus felt about Jairus's request? (2)
. . . the crowd felt when Jesus followed Jairus? (3)
. . . the seriously ill woman felt? (4)
. . . Jairus felt as Jesus delayed to help the woman? (5)
. . . the mourners felt when Jesus told them the girl was sleeping? (6)
. . . Jairus and his wife felt when Jesus gave them their daughter? (7)
. . . the blind men felt when they heard Jesus was coming? (8)
. . . the blind men felt when Jesus ignored them? (9)
. . . the blind men felt when Jesus healed them? (10)
. . . Jesus felt when He went to bed at night and knew there were people still in pain whom His power could have healed? (11)
How do you feel when you encounter a need? (12)

Place the heading on the wall and call on the person you have enlisted **IN ADVANCE** to read all of the Scripture at this point. Place the first question under the heading and ask members to respond. Using the material in "Studying the Bible," explain who Jairus was.

Place the second poster under the first poster. Ask, Do you think Jesus ever got tired of people coming to Him for help?

Place the third poster on the wall. Ask, Was the crowd surprised to see Jesus follow this man?

Place the fourth poster on the wall. Use the material in "Studying the Bible" to explain how isolating this woman's disease was and why she was reluctant to confront Jesus openly for healing.

Place the fifth question on the wall and ask members to respond.

Place the sixth question on the wall. Use the material in "Studying the Bible" to explain the role of professional mourners.

Place the seventh question on the wall and ask members to respond to how Jairus and his wife felt.

Place the eighth poster on the wall and ask members to respond.

Place the ninth poster on the wall and ask members to respond. Use the material in "Studying the Bible" to explain why Jesus may not have responded immediately.

Place the tenth poster on the wall and ask members to respond by using only one word.

Place the eleventh poster on the wall and ask members to respond.

Give the Truth a Personal Focus

Read the six "Summary of Bible Truths" statements. Begin by saying, "This lesson teaches us that we . . . ." Tape the twelfth poster on the wall over the rest of the statements and ask members to respond to that question in light of the lesson. Ask members to identify persons to whom they can show compassion this week.

1. Tennessee Williams, *A Streetcar Named Desire,* 1947.
2. R. Wayne Willis, Louisville, Kentucky.
3. Laurie Tarkan, "Teaching Kids Compassion," *Good Housekeeping,* Oct. 1996, 166.
4. Anna Quindlen, *Redbook,* May 1994, 38.

January 23, 2000

Opposition to Jesus

Background Passage: Matthew 12:22–45
Focal Passages: Matthew 12:22–32, 38–40

Jesus was moved with compassion when He saw the crowds, but the religious leaders were moved with jealous rage when they saw Jesus. They saw Him as a threat to their positions. They were frustrated by their attempts to discredit Him in the eyes of the people. Therefore, their attacks became more vicious and reckless.

▶**Study Aim:** *To describe two examples of opposition to Jesus and how He responded to each.*

STUDYING THE BIBLE

OUTLINE AND SUMMARY

I. **Accusing Jesus of Using Satan's Power (Matt. 12:22–37)**
 1. Reckless accusation (12:22–24)
 2. Miracles wrought by the Spirit's power (12:25–29)
 3. No neutrals in the cosmic struggle (12:30)
 4. The unpardonable sin (12:31, 32)
 5. Warning of judgment (12:33–37)

II. **Demanding That Jesus Give Them a Sign (Matt. 12:38–45)**
 1. Request for a sign (12:38)
 2. Sign of Jonah (12:39–42)
 3. Danger of spiritual emptiness (12:43–45)

After Jesus performed an exorcism, the Pharisees accused Him of using Satan's power (vv. 22–24). Jesus said that God's Spirit, not Satan, was at war with evil (vv. 25–29). In this cosmic struggle, one is either with Jesus or against Him (v. 30). He warned the Pharisees about a sin for which there is no pardon (vv. 31, 32). Judgment is sure on evil hearts, which overflow with evil fruit and evil words (vv. 33–37). The Pharisees asked Jesus to show them a sign (v. 38). He warned against demanding signs and told them that the only sign would be that of Jonah (vv. 39–42). An empty heart or life will be filled by evil if not by God (vv. 43–45).

I. Accusing Jesus of Using Satan's Power (Matt. 12:22–37)

1. Reckless accusation (vv. 22–24)

22 Then was brought unto him one possessed with a devil, blind, and dumb: and he healed him, insomuch that the blind and dumb both spake and saw.

23 And all the people were amazed, and said, Is not this the son of David?

24 But when the Pharisees heard it, they said, This fellow doth not cast out devils, but by Beelzebub the prince of the devils.

The man's basic problem was that he was possessed by a demon. In his case, this problem was accompanied by the man's inability to see or to hear. When Jesus exorcised the demon, the man was able to speak and see. The astonished people wondered if Jesus might be the Messiah (son of David) for whom they were looking.

The angry Pharisees could not deny that a miracle had taken place; therefore, they made a reckless charge against Jesus in an attempt to discredit Jesus in the eyes of the people. They accused Jesus of casting out the demon by the power of Beelzebub. Explanations for the derivation of the name vary, but the name means "lord of the flies" and became another name for Satan, who was the prince of evil spirits.

2. Miracles wrought by the Spirit's power (vv. 25–29)

25 And Jesus knew their thoughts, and said unto them, Every kingdom divided against itself is brought to desolation; and every city or house divided against itself shall not stand:

26 And if Satan cast out Satan, he is divided against himself; how shall then his kingdom stand?

27 And if I by Beelzebub cast out devils, by whom do your children cast them out? therefore they shall be your judges.

Jesus began His response with an obvious fact of human life and history. When a nation engages in a civil war, the result is the desolation of the country. When a city is divided into warring factions or a family is divided by infighting, the city or the family cannot survive as a healthy functioning unit of society. By the same token, Satan's domain cannot survive if Satan wages war against himself by casting out some of his evil forces. Therefore, the charge that Satan would help Jesus or anyone else cast out demons makes absolutely no sense.

Some of the Pharisees were exorcists who claimed they had power to cast out evil spirits. Jesus asked if they also were using Satan's power to perform exorcisms. If Jesus was casting out demons by Satan's power, it was only logical to assume that all exorcists also relied on the devil's power. The Pharisees certainly were not willing to make such a charge against their own.

28 But if I cast out devils by the Spirit of God, then the kingdom of God is come unto you.

29 Or else how can one enter into a strong man's house, and spoil his goods, except he first bind the strong man? and then he will spoil his house.

Jesus then forced His attackers to face the logical answer to the question, "By what power does Jesus cast out demons?" If Jesus did not rely on Satan for His power, He relied on the power of the Holy Spirit—the true enemy of Satan. If He was casting out demons by the Spirit's power, then this was one of many signs that the kingdom of God had come.

Verse 29 uses a human analogy to reinforce Christ as the victor over Satan. If a strong man's house is robbed while the strong man is at home, the intruder must overcome and render helpless the strong man. In this short illustration, Satan is the strong man; and Jesus is the One who overcomes and binds the strong man.

This passage deals with three important Bible doctrines: the Holy Spirit, Christ's victory over Satan, and the kingdom of God.

1. In earlier lessons in Matthew, we saw the Spirit's work in the miraculous conception (1:20), One who would baptize with the Holy Spirit (3:11), when Jesus was baptized (3:16), and the temptations (4:1). The Spirit was the power by which Jesus cast out demons.

2. Jesus' work is portrayed as a victory over Satan. His victory over temptation was part of this victory (Matt. 4:11). Casting out demons was a sign of His victory. His death and resurrection delivered mortal blows to Satan (John 12:31; Heb. 2:14, 15).

3. The kingdom of God was revealed in Jesus' coming, life, death, and resurrection. Jesus also taught His followers to pray, "Thy kingdom come" (Matt. 6:10). The kingdom of God came in Jesus Christ's victory over Satan, sin, and death; however, the consummation of that kingdom has not yet taken place.

3. No neutrals in the cosmic struggle (v. 30)

> 30 He that is not with me is against me; and he that gathereth not with me scattereth abroad.

Verses 22–29 make clear that a cosmic struggle was raging during Jesus' ministry. The rest of the New Testament makes clear that the struggle continues. Satan has received a mortal blow that dooms him and all who follow him; but like a mortally wounded animal, he viciously attacks everything in sight (1 Pet. 5:8). In such a cosmic struggle between God and Satan, no one can be neutral. Those who claim to be neutral are actually on Satan's side. This is the point of the strong words of Jesus in verse 30.

In Matthew 9:36–38, Jesus used two analogies to describe His work and that of His followers. He is the Good Shepherd who seeks the lost sheep who are scattered. He calls His followers to pray for workers in a vast harvest field. The words *gathereth* and *scattereth abroad* may reflect either of these. If we are not helping gather in the scattered flock or engaged in gathering in the vast harvest, we are not really with Christ; for these are His priorities. And if we are not with Him, we are against Him.

4. The unpardonable sin (vv. 31, 32)

> 31 Wherefore I say unto you, All manner of sin and blasphemy shall be forgiven unto men: but the blasphemy against the Holy Ghost shall not be forgiven unto men.
>
> 32 And whosoever speaketh a word against the Son of man, it shall be forgiven him: but whosoever speaketh against the Holy Ghost, it shall not be forgiven him, neither in this world, neither in the world to come.

By focusing exclusively on the unpardonable sin in this passage, we often fail to notice the promises of forgiveness of all other sins. Except for this one sin, "all manner of sin and blasphemy shall be forgiven unto men." This includes words spoken against the Son of man. Jesus prayed on the cross for those who crucified Him (Luke 23:34). The heart of God yearns to forgive sinners; only when people make that impossible is God unable to forgive.

Considerable discussion swirls around what Jesus meant by the sin that "shall not be forgiven." Whatever it was, it was committed by people opposed to Jesus, not His followers. It also had to do with rejecting God's revelation in Christ as signified by the power of God's Spirit.

The most narrow interpretation limits the unpardonable sin to attributing the work of the Holy Spirit to Satan. This was how the sin was expressed in this specific situation. However, many people see this as only one expression of a broader sin—that of persistently rejecting God's revelation of Himself in Christ as the Spirit convicts people of sin and seeks to point them to Jesus.

This broader interpretation is consistent with other Bible passages. After all, the work of the Spirit is to glorify Christ, not call attention to Himself (John 16:13, 14). Persistently refusing to believe in Christ in the full light of God's revelation is to choose darkness rather than light (John 3:17–21; 9:37–41). The Pharisees knew that Jesus was God's Son; yet they rejected Him in the full light of that knowledge. Thus, the unpardonable sin is refusing God's offer of pardon.

5. Warning of judgment (vv. 33–37)

The human heart is the source of evil, and those whose hearts are evil bear evil fruit in their lives and speak evil words with their tongues (vv. 33–35). Such evil people will not escape sure judgment for their evil hearts, lives, and words (vv. 36, 37).

II. Demanding That Jesus Give Them a Sign (Matt. 12:38–45)

1. Request for a sign (v. 38)

> **38 Then certain of the scribes and of the Pharisees answered, saying, Master, we would see a sign from thee.**

A "sign" was different from an ordinary miracle. There were a number of miracle workers around, but the Pharisees requested a sure sign from heaven that Jesus was who He claimed to be.

2. Sign of Jonah (vv. 39–42)

> **39 But he answered and said unto them, An evil and adulterous generation seeketh after a sign; and there shall no sign be given to it, but the sign of the prophet Jonas:**
>
> **40 For as Jonas was three days and three nights in the whale's belly; so shall the Son of man be three days and three nights in the heart of the earth.**

Demanding that Jesus prove Himself by a special sign from heaven is evidence of the arrogant unbelief of the people who make such a demand. Jesus labeled the sign seekers "an evil and adulterous generation." Jesus knew that their hearts were so evil that they would not accept a sign, even if it were given. (For examples, see Luke 16:31; John 11:46–53; Matt. 28:11–15.)

This was in fact the only sign Jesus said they would be given—the sign of Jonah (Jonas). Jesus' reference to Jonah and the great fish foreshadowed the death, burial, and resurrection of Jesus. Sinners today have the word of this good news brought to bear on their hearts by the Spirit. Sadly, many reject as did so many in Jesus' day.

Repentant sinners of earlier generations will condemn those who reject the full revelation of God in Christ. These will include the evil people of pagan Nineveh who repented at the preaching of a reluctant Jonah and the queen of Sheba who came to see the wisdom of Solomon. Jonah and Solomon were pale shadows of the One who is so much greater than any other (vv. 41, 42).

3. Danger of spiritual emptiness (vv. 43–45)

Jesus compared that evil generation to a person who had gotten rid of one evil spirit only to have that spirit return along with seven worse spirits. A person or a nation must do more than get rid of its evils. An empty heart will soon be invaded by old and new evils unless God is allowed into a cleansed heart and life.

PRONUNCIATION GUIDE

Beelzebub	[bee EL zee buhb]
Nineveh	[NIN uh vuh]
Sheba	[SHEE bah]

SUMMARY OF BIBLE TRUTHS

1. Jesus, the Son of God, has power over evil.
2. Casting out demons was one sign of Jesus' victory over Satan.
3. The miracles of Jesus were signs of the coming of God's kingdom.
4. Stubborn resistance to the Spirit makes a person unpardonable.
5. One evidence of a hardened heart is a demand for God to give a special sign.
6. Stubborn unbelief would not be changed even if a sign were given.

APPLYING THE BIBLE

1. Jealousy and jaundice. John Dryden called jealousy the "jaundice of the soul."[1] Those who oppose Jesus do so because they are spiritually jaundiced.

2. Too much self-love. In jealousy there is more self-love than love.[2] The opposition to Jesus comes from those who are drowning in self-love. They oppose Jesus to protect their own interest, not for their love for God.

3. Hardened hearts. In the devotional classic *My Utmost for His Highest* Oswald Chambers says, "Never try to explain God until you have obeyed him." The hardened hearts of the Pharisees were evidence that they had not obeyed God with the matters of the heart. Not only could they not explain Him; they couldn't recognize Him in the person of His Son.

4. Wrong signs. The signs that people want from God are usually spectacular signs, not the signs that speak to the heart about the person of Christ. Woody Allen may well summarize an entire generation of sign seekers when he says, "If only God would give me some clear sign! Like making a large deposit in my name at a Swiss bank."

5. John's seven signs. The Gospel of John records seven signs of Jesus, each one intended to demonstrate something of Jesus' character.

Sign	Demonstration
Changing water into wine	Jesus is the source of our joy
Healing a nobleman's son	Jesus is the source of our hope
Healing a lame man	Jesus is the source of our strength
Feeding 5,000 with a boy's lunch	Jesus is the supplier of our deepest need
Calming a storm	Jesus is the source of our courage
Healing a man born blind	Jesus is the source of our vision
Raising Lazarus from the dead	Jesus is the source of our life

God had given all the signs necessary, especially to those who knew the Hebrew Scriptures, but they refused to believe.

6. Don't miss the signs. When we miss the signs that are intended for our good, three things can happen: (1) We do not arrive at our desired destination; we are lost instead. (2) We are in danger of getting hurt; signs warn us of danger. (3) We will live with regret; missing a sign always has consequences.

TEACHING THE BIBLE

- *Main Idea:* People who did not want to accept Jesus opposed Him.
- *Suggested Teaching Aim:* To lead adults to accept Jesus rather than oppose Him.

A TEACHING OUTLINE

Accusing Jesus of Using Satan's Power (Matt. 12:22–37)
Reckless accusation (vv. 22–24)
Miracles wrought by the Spirit's power (vv. 25–29)
No neutrals in the cosmic struggle (v. 30)
The unpardonable sin (vv. 31–32)
Warning of judgment (vv. 33–37)
Demanding That Jesus Give Them a Sign (Matt. 12:38–45)
Request for a sign (v. 38)
Sign of Jonah (vv. 39–42)
Danger of spiritual emptiness (vv. 43–45)

January 23, 2000

Introduce the Bible Study

Use number 3, "Hardened Hearts," in "Applying the Bible" to introduce the lesson.

Search for Biblical Truth

IN ADVANCE, enlist a member to read aloud the summary statements in "Outline and Summary" to overview the Scripture passages. Call for the reading now.

Present a lecture, using the material in "Studying the Bible." Copy the above outline on strips of paper or write it on a chalkboard. Place the first point ("I. Accusing Jesus of Using Satan's Power [Matt. 12:22–27]") and the first subpoint ("1. Reckless accusation [vv. 22–24]") on the focal wall. **IN ADVANCE,** enlist a member to read the Scripture. Ask for Matthew 12:22–24 to be read at this time. Lecture briefly:

- Jesus healed a man possessed with a devil, and the people were amazed.
- The Pharisees accused Jesus of casting the demon out by using Beelzebub's power.
- Place the second subpoint on the wall ("2. Miracles wrought by the Spirit's power [vv. 25–29]"). Ask for this Scripture to be read aloud. Lecture briefly on these points:
- When a nation engages in a civil war, the result is a desolation of the country.
- Likewise, Satan's domain could not survive if Satan fought against himself.
- If Jesus cast out demons by Satan's power, all the exorcists must also rely on that power; the Pharisees were unwilling to admit that.
- Jesus used God's Spirit to cast out demons; this proves God's kingdom has come.
- Comment briefly on the three important Bible doctrines in this passage: (1) the Holy Spirit, (2) Christ's victory over Satan, and (3) the kingdom of God.

Place the third subpoint on the wall ("3. No neutrals in the cosmic struggle [v. 30]") and lecture briefly:

- No one can be neutral in this struggle between good and evil.
- Write on a chalkboard: *Not to choose is to choose* and ask members to respond.
- How can we know whose side we are on? If we are not helping gather in the scattered flock or the vast harvest (Matt. 9:36–38), we are not really with Christ.

Place the fourth subpoint on the wall ("4. The unpardonable sin [vv. 31–32]") and ask the reader to read verses 31–32. Lecture briefly:

- Emphasize that these verses contain the promise to forgive all sin but one.
- The heart of God yearns to forgive sinners; only when people make that impossible is God unable to forgive.
- Present the narrow and broad interpretations of the unpardonable sin.

Place the second main point ("II. Demanding That Jesus Give Them a Sign [Matt. 12:38–45]") and the first subpoint ("1. Request for a sign [v. 38]") on the wall. Ask the reader to read verse 38; explain how a sign differs from a miracle.

Place the second subpoint ("2. Sign of Jonah [vv. 39–42]") on the wall and ask the reader to read verses 39–40. Lecture briefly:
- Demanding a sign indicates arrogant unbelief.
- Share number 4, "Wrong Signs," in "Applying the Bible."
- What the sign of Jonah would reveal to all people.

Place the third subpoint on the wall ("3. Danger of spiritual emptiness [vv. 43–45]") and ask the reader to read these verses. Summarize these verses by saying: "An empty heart will soon be invaded by old and new evils unless God is allowed into a cleansed heart and life."

Give the Truth a Personal Focus

Read each of the six "Summary of Bible Truths" and ask, What relationship does this truth have to our lives?

---
1. John Dryden, "The Hind and the Panther" [1687], pt. III, l. 73.
2. François, Duc de La Rochefoucauld.

Laborers in the Vineyard

January 30, 2000

Background Passage: Matthew 19:16–20:16
Focal Passage: Matthew 20:1–16

The laborers in the vineyard is one of the most difficult parables to understand. Evidence of this is seen in the many and varied interpretations of Jesus' story. The problem in Matthew 20:1–16 is why the employer paid all his workers the same, no matter how long they worked, and what this has to do with the saying that the last will be first, and the first, last.

▶**Study Aim:** *To explain the parable of the laborers in the vineyard.*

STUDYING THE BIBLE

OUTLINE AND SUMMARY

I. **Renouncing All to Follow Jesus (Matt. 19:16–30)**
   1. **The young man's refusal (19:16–22)**
   2. **Who then can be saved? (19:23–26)**
   3. **Rewards for renunciation (19:27–30)**

II. **Parable of the Laborers in the Vineyard (Matt. 20:1–16)**
   1. **A parable of the kingdom (20:1–7)**
   2. **Grumbling about pay (20:8–12)**
   3. **The owner's fairness and generosity (20:13–16)**

The young man refused to give up his riches and depend on God (19:16–22). Jesus said that the rich cannot be saved by human means, but only by God's grace and power (19:23–26). When Peter asked about their reward, Jesus described divine blessings but added a word of caution (19:27–30). Jesus told of a vineyard keeper who hired workers at five different times during the day, promising the first group a denarius (20:1–7). When the last group was paid a denarius, the first group grumbled (20:8–12). The employer said that he had acted fairly, freely, and generously (20:13–16).

I. Renouncing All to Follow Jesus (Matt. 19:16–30)

1. The young man's refusal (19:16–22)

A young man asked Jesus what good thing he could do to inherit eternal life (19:16). When Jesus spoke to him about the Commandments, the man claimed to have kept them (19:17–20). Jesus challenged him to sell everything and give it to the poor (19:21). The young man had many possessions and was not willing to give them up in order to follow Jesus (19:22).

2. Who then can be saved? (19:23–26)

Jesus told the disciples that it is humanly impossible for a rich man to be saved (19:23, 24). The surprised disciples asked, "Who then can be saved?" (19:25). Jesus said that the rich person can be saved only by the grace and power of God (19:26).

3. Rewards for renunciation (19:27–30)

Noting the disciple's renunciation of all things to follow Jesus, Peter asked, "What shall we have therefore?" (19:27). Jesus gave a twofold answer to Peter's question: First, Jesus assured the disciples that their renunciation would result in divine blessings (19:28, 29). Second, Jesus warned, "Many that are first shall be last; and the last shall be first" (19:30).

II. Parable of the Laborers in the Vineyard (Matt. 20:1–16)

1. A parable of the kingdom (20:1–7)

> **1 For the kingdom of heaven is like unto a man that is an householder, which went out early in the morning to hire labourers into his vineyard.**

The parable begins like so many of Jesus' parables in Matthew's Gospel (see 13:24, 44, 45, 47; 25:1). In other words, Jesus told this story to illustrate some reality in our relation to God as our King. As you seek to understand this parable, keep in mind these facts about Jesus' parables.

1. People in Jesus' parables often acted in ways that people normally would not act. The "householder" was a man who owned a house and vineyard. In some ways, he acted like any vineyard owner; but in other ways, Jesus portrayed the man as acting very differently.

2. Most parables were designed to make one point, not to be allegories in which every detail represents something in God's kingdom.

3. The context is the key to many parables. Jesus told this story as an explanation of Matthew 19:30, which was part of His answer to Peter's question about rewards. The repetition of Matthew 19:30 in 20:16 shows this connection between Matthew 19:16–30 and Matthew 20:1–16.

> **2 And when he had agreed with the labourers for a penny a day, he sent them into his vineyard.**
>
> **3 And he went out about the third hour, and saw others standing idle in the marketplace,**
>
> **4 And said unto them; Go ye also into the vineyard, and whatsoever is right I will give you. And they went their way.**
>
> **5 Again he went out about the sixth and ninth hour, and did likewise.**
>
> **6 And about the eleventh hour he went out, and found others standing idle, and saith unto them, Why stand ye here all the day idle?**
>
> **7 They say unto him, Because no man hath hired us. He saith unto them, Go ye also into the vineyard; and whatsoever is right, that shall ye receive.**

The Jews defined the first hour of the day as the first hour after sunrise. Thus, the third hour would be about 9:00 A.M. The sixth hour was

January 30, 2000

noon. The ninth hour was about 3:00 P.M. The eleventh hour was about 5:00 P.M.

The vineyard owner began the day as did any man in his position. During harvest season, vineyard owners hired extra workers to pick grapes. Therefore, the man went early to the marketplace where such workers gathered in hope of being hired for the day. He hired workers and promised to pay them a denarius ("penny"), which was a coin equal to pay for a day's work of picking grapes. The workers agreed and went to the vineyard and began working.

For some reason, the vineyard owner returned for more workers four other times during the day. The story does not explain why he did not hire all he needed at the beginning of the day. Jesus built into his story this repeated return in order to make a point about service to God. Jesus' vineyard owner did not act as most owners acted. Most would have hired all they needed at the beginning.

The word translated "idle" means literally "without work" or "unemployed." At times this word is used in the New Testament to mean "lazy" (Titus 1:12), but in Matthew 20:3, 6, "idle" means "unemployed." When the last group was asked why they stood idle all day, they replied, "Because no man hath hired us."

The vineyard owner did not promise to pay the later groups a denarius, as he had the first group. Instead, he told the group at 9:00 A.M. that he would pay them what was right. Apparently he made the same statement to each group hired.

2. Grumbling about pay (20:8–12)

> **8 So when even was come, the lord of the vineyard saith unto his steward, Call the labourers, and give them their hire, beginning from the last unto the first.**
>
> **9 And when they came that were hired about the eleventh hour, they received every man a penny.**
>
> **10 But when the first came, they supposed that they should have received more; and they likewise received every man a penny.**
>
> **11 And when they had received it, they murmured against the goodman of the house,**
>
> **12 Saying, These last have wrought but one hour, and thou hast made them equal unto us, which have borne the burden and heat of the day.**

Paying this kind of workers at the end of each work day was normal, and the owner instructed his steward to distribute the pay. However, he gave the steward instructions that were not typical of vineyard owners. He told the steward to begin paying the last group first. Normally, the ones longest in the fields would be paid first. The owner also told the steward to pay everyone a denarius. Normally, an owner would pay people based on how long they worked.

Jesus was not giving instructions about how to pay workers. Employees expect to be paid for the work they have done; and if they are hourly employees, they expect to be paid according to the hours worked. Extra work deserves extra pay. Jesus deliberately had this employer pay the last first and pay everyone the same.

Jesus told the story to make a point about God and those who serve Him. In a human situation, the early workers' grievance was predictable and probably justified. However, in our relationship with God, people act sinfully when they insist on getting what they deserve and complaining about what they receive from God. As anyone saved by grace knows, we would be in real trouble if God truly gave us what we deserved. We can be glad that He relates to us with mercy and grace.

3. The owner's fairness and generosity (20:13–16)

> 13 But he answered one of them, and said, Friend, I do thee no wrong: didst not thou agree with me for a penny?
>
> 14 Take that thine is, and go thy way: I will give unto this last, even as unto thee.
>
> 15 Is it not lawful for me to do what I will with mine own? Is thine eye evil, because I am good?
>
> 16 So the last shall be first, and the first last: for many be called, but few chosen.

The owner's response was directed to one, who apparently was the spokesman for the group. If we assume the owner represents God, his response highlights several facts about God, His relationship to us, and our responses to Him.

God is like Jesus' vineyard owner in at least three ways:

1. Because He is God, He has the right to do whatever He chooses to do. Thus, the vineyard owner insisted that he was free to do as he pleased with what was his.
2. God chooses to be fair or just. This is seen in verse 13. The employer hired the first workers for a denarius, and he paid them what He had promised.
3. God is more than fair; He is generous. He chooses to give more than we deserve. The late workers had trusted the owner's word to do what was right. What he chose to do was to be generous with them.

The early workers were angry at the man who had hired them and begrudged what the man gave so generously to the late workers. An "evil eye" was used at times to refer to looking on someone with malice and evil intent. This may be its meaning in Mark 7:22. At other times, as in Deuteronomy 15:9 and probably in Matthew 6:23, it was used to describe greedy people who begrudged sharing anything of theirs with others. Both ideas may be implied in verse 15 because the early workers were angry with the employer and begrudged his generosity to the late workers.

Some people see their relation with God as a bargain in which God gives them what they deserve. Such people seldom experience His goodness, grace, and generosity. They are too busy complaining if they are not properly rewarded for their service. Peter had not complained, but his question implied that the faithful service of the disciples deserved something special. He had either forgotten or never learned that Christians'

January 30, 2000

relationship with God is based on grace. This applies not only to salvation but also to service.

The only human response to God that enables one to enter the kingdom is a sense of dependence on God. Only the "poor in spirit" enter the kingdom (Matt. 5:3), and only the humble are great in the kingdom (Matt. 20:17–28). The problem with the rich young ruler was that he was unwilling to come to God as a sinner, poor and needy. He wanted to be rewarded for his obedience to the Commandments. When Jesus placed him in a situation in which he would have to trust God completely, he was unwilling to do that.

Peter left all to follow Christ, but he continued to harbor worldly ideas about prominence in the kingdom. Jesus was reminding him that although faithfulness results in blessings, these are not rewards for what Peter had done; they are gifts of God's grace. Thus, "blessings" is a better word than "rewards," which implies that we deserve the rewards because of what we have done.

Peter and the disciples thought of themselves as "first." Matthew 20:17–28 shows that they often argued among themselves about which of them was first or greatest. People who assume that rewards are based on human merit grumble against God and struggle with others in a competitive way for prominence in the kingdom. Jesus told this story to show that anyone who considers himself "first" for these mistaken reasons will be disappointed. Those who are willing to place themselves "last" in prominence by humble, self-giving service are "first" in God's eyes.

PRONUNCIATION GUIDE

denarius   [dee NAHR ih uhs]

SUMMARY OF BIBLE TRUTHS

1. God shows His sovereignty by being not only fair but also generous.
2. God's grace, not human merit, is the basis for our relationship with Him and service in His name.
3. Faithfulness brings divine blessings, based on His grace, not rewards based on what we deserve.
4. People who insist on getting what they deserve will inevitably be disappointed.
5. Seeking to be first is characteristic of worldly standards, not kingdom standards.
6. Proper human responses to God include dependence, trust, gratitude, contentment, faithfulness, and humility.

APPLYING THE BIBLE

1. Fair pay. In a recent article titled "Musicians Finally Get What They Deserve," the Kingsmen were awarded a court decision that says they are entitled to thirty years' worth of royalties for the song "Louie Louie." Since a contract was signed in 1968, the group was supposed to

January 30 2000

receive 9 percent of the profits or licensing fees from the record. After thirty years, they finally got what they deserved.

Life does not always seem fair. However, one thing is certain: God has a way of balancing the scales! He is fair. The vineyard owner treated his workers fairly. A day's wage was promised to all who worked in the vineyard. We may feel that we deserve more at times than other people, but that is not the case. Salvation is a gift. No one deserves it, but God is equally gracious to all whom He calls.

2. He went away sad. The rich young man was possessed by his possessions. "There is enough for the needy but not for the greedy" (Mohandas K. Gandhi).

3. Greed. Clovis Chappell wrote in his book of sermons *Feminine Faces:* "When Pompeii was being excavated, there was found a body that had been embalmed by the ashes of Vesuvius. It was that of a woman. Her feet were turned toward the city gate, but her face was turned backward toward something that lay just beyond her outstretched hands. The prize for which those frozen fingers were reaching was a bag of pearls. Maybe she herself had dropped them as she was fleeing for her life. Maybe she had found them where they had been dropped by another. But, be that as it may, though death was hard at her heels, and life was beckoning to her beyond the city gates, she could not shake off their spell. She had turned to pick them up, with death as her reward. But it was not the eruption of Vesuvius that made her love pearls more than life. It only froze her in this attitude of greed."

4. God's nature. Third- and fourth-graders at Wheaton Christian Grammar School in Illinois were asked to complete the following sentence: "By faith, I know that God is . . ."

"**forgiving**, because he forgave in the Bible, and he forgave me when I went in the road on my bike without one of my parents" (Amanda).

"**providingful**, because he dropped manna for Moses and the people, and he gave my dad a job" (Brandon).

"**caring**, because he made the blind man see, and he made me catch a very fast line drive that could have hurt me. He probably sent an angel down" (Paul).

"**merciful**, because my brother has been nice to me for a year" (Jeremy).

"**faithful**, because the school bill came, and my mom didn't know how we were going to pay it. Two minutes later, my dad called, and he just got a bonus check. My mom was in tears" (anonymous).

"**sweet**, because he gave me a dog. God tells me not to do things that are bad. I need someone like that" (Hannah).

5. A prayer for generosity:
>Teach us, good Lord, to serve Thee as Thou deservest:
>To give and not to count the cost;
>To fight and not to heed the wounds;
>To toil and not to seek for rest;
>To labor and not ask for any reward
>Save that of knowing that we do Thy will.
>—Ignatius of Loyola

January

30

2000

TEACHING THE BIBLE

- *Main Idea:* Jesus said we all get into heaven by God's grace.
- *Suggested Teaching Aim:* To lead these adults to accept and share God's grace.

A TEACHING OUTLINE

1. Renouncing All to Follow Jesus (Matt. 19:16–30)
2. Parable of the Laborers in the Vineyard (Matt. 20:1–16)

Introduce the Bible Study

Use number 1, "Fair Pay," in "Applying the Bible" to introduce the lesson.

Search for Biblical Truth

IN ADVANCE, enlist three people to read the comments in "Studying the Bible" on "I. Renouncing All to Follow Jesus." Copy the three paragraphs and distribute to three people to set the context out of which Jesus told the parable of the laborers. Ask members to listen for why Jesus told this parable after the experience with the man we sometimes call the rich young ruler.

IN ADVANCE, copy the six questions in "Give the Truth a Personal Focus" and give to six members of your class. Distribute these to six members or six groups at the beginning of the class and ask them to listen throughout the lesson and form an answer and share at the conclusion of the study.

Ask members to open their Bibles to Matthew 20:1–16 and scan these verses. Use the three statements in "Studying the Bible" to explain Jesus' use of parables.

If you have members with modern translations, ask them to determine what times the owner of the vineyard went out to hire laborers. (9:00, 3:00, and 5:00.) Also ask them if they can determine how much the workers were paid. (Most translations have something like the "normal or usual wage," possibly "minimum wage.") Ask: Why do you think the men went to work later in the day without knowing what wage they would receive? Why did the owner not tell them?

DISCUSS: How is God like the vineyard owner? (See "Studying the Bible.")

Give the Truth a Personal Focus

IN ADVANCE, copy the six questions in "Give the Truth a Personal Focus" and give to six members of your class. Distribute these to members at the beginning of the class and ask them to form an answer and share it.

Read each of the following questions (based on the "Summary of Bible Truths") and let members respond:

- How does God show that He is not only fair but also generous?

January 30 2000

- What evidence can you give that God's grace, not human merit, is the basis for our relationship with God and service in His name?
- Why does God base His blessings on His grace and not on rewards based on what we deserve?
- Why do you think people who insist on getting what they deserve will inevitably be disappointed?
- If seeking to be first is characteristic of worldly standards, not kingdom standards, why do so many who call themselves believers seek to be first?
- Which of the proper human responses to God (dependence, trust, gratitude, contentment, faithfulness, and humility) do you need to develop in your life?

Close in prayer that members may be able to accept *and* share God's grace.

February 6, 2000

Coming to Jerusalem

Background Passage: Matthew 21:1–17
Focal Passage: Matthew 21:1–13

The Old Testament prophets sometimes did unusual things to clarify or reinforce their spoken words. This is called prophetic symbolism. In connection with Jesus' final coming to Jerusalem, He did two acts of prophetic symbolism: His unusual entry into the city and His bold actions in the temple.

▶**Study Aim:** *To recognize what Jesus' royal entry and cleansing the temple reveal about His identity and mission.*

STUDYING THE BIBLE

OUTLINE AND SUMMARY

I. **Royal Entry into Jerusalem (Matt. 21:1–11)**
  1. **Came as the meek King (21:1–7)**
  2. **Acclaimed as the Son of David (21:8, 9)**
  3. **Created a great stir (21:10, 11)**

II. **Cleansing the Temple (Matt. 21:12–17)**
  1. **Attacked the money-makers (21:12)**
  2. **Condemned making the temple into a den of thieves (21:13)**
  3. **Aroused the anger of the chief priests (21:14–17)**

Jesus entered Jerusalem in a way to reveal Him as a humble Messiah (vv. 1–7). The people acclaimed Jesus as the Son of David (vv. 8, 9). His entry created a great stir throughout the city (vv. 10, 11). Jesus went into the temple and drove out the money changers and sellers of animals (v. 12). He accused them of making God's house of prayer into a den of thieves (v. 13). His actions in the temple made the chief priests very angry at Jesus (vv. 14–17).

I. Royal Entry into Jerusalem (Matt. 21:1–11)

1. Came as the meek King (vv. 1–7)

1 And when they drew nigh unto Jerusalem, and were come to Bethphage, unto the mount of Olives, then sent Jesus two disciples,

2 Saying unto them, Go into the village over against you, and straightway ye shall find an ass tied, and a colt with her: loose them, and bring them unto me.

3 And if any man say ought unto you, ye shall say, The Lord hath need of them; and straightway he will send them.

4 All this was done, that it might be fulfilled which was spoken by the prophet, saying,

5 Tell ye the daughter of Sion, Behold, thy King cometh unto thee, meek, and sitting upon an ass, and a colt the foal of an ass.

6 And the disciples went, and did as Jesus commanded them,

7 And brought the ass, and the colt, and put on them their clothes, and they set him thereon.

As Jesus prepared to enter Jerusalem for the final time, He gave instructions to two of His disciples. They were to enter a village (probably Bethphage), find a female donkey and her colt, and bring them to Jesus. The Lord told the disciples what to say if anyone questioned what they were doing. The two disciples followed Jesus' instructions, brought the animals to Jesus, spread their robes on the animals as a saddle, and set Jesus on the colt.

Verses 4, 5 emphasize that this action fulfilled Zechariah 9:9. The first line of the quotation probably reflects Isaiah 62:11. Zechariah 9:9 was considered by many Jews to relate to the coming of the Messiah-King. Jesus deliberately chose to fulfill that particular Old Testament promise because it describes the King as "meek," a word Jesus used of Himself in Matthew 11:29, and a word He used in one of the Beatitudes to describe kingdom citizens (Matt. 5:5). Jesus did not enter Jerusalem as a military and political King, riding a white horse and dressed as a king and warrior. He entered as a humble Servant-King.

Throughout His ministry, Jesus had faced a dilemma about how to reveal Himself as Messiah-King. From the beginning of Matthew, He is called the Christ (Messiah), the Son of David (1:1). Yet He had come to save His people from sin, not from the power of Roman domination (Matt. 1:21). To fulfill this mission involved crucifixion and resurrection. Jesus committed Himself to such a mission, and the Father's words at Jesus' baptism indicate His approval (Matt. 3:17).

The problem was that many of the Jewish people were expecting an earthly king. Even Jesus' disciples were expecting an earthly king. When Jesus began clearly to predict His rejection, suffering, death, and resurrection, Peter rebuked Jesus for saying such a thing (Matt. 16:13–25). Although Jesus continued to predict what was to happen in Jerusalem, the disciples did not understand. Even as they approached Jerusalem, the Twelve were arguing about which of them would be the greatest (Matt. 20:17–28).

2. Acclaimed as the Son of David (vv. 8, 9)

8 And a very great multitude spread their garments in the way; others cut down branches from the trees, and strawed them in the way.

9 And the multitudes that went before, and that followed, cried, saying, Hosanna to the son of David: Blessed is he that cometh in the name of the Lord; Hosanna in the highest.

Jesus was taking a calculated risk by entering Jerusalem as the Messiah. He came as King, but as a humble Servant-King, not as a mighty political king. However, the people failed to note this subtle difference.

February 6, 2000

Verses 8, 9 show that they disregarded the humility depicted by riding on a donkey colt and the word *meek* in Zechariah 9:9. All they saw was a King, their kind of king, one worthy of being called Son of David, the great warrior king of their glorious past.

Jesus entered Jerusalem during Passover season (Matt. 26:2). At this most famous of Jewish feasts, the city was always crowded with Jews from many places. Expectations of the Messiah ran high at Passover. As Jesus passed through Jericho, crowds were already with Him (Matt. 20:29). As Jesus approached the city, others joined the throngs about Him. By the time He rode into Jerusalem, Jesus had crowds in front of Him and behind Him. They were placing their cloaks in front of Him and paving the road with branches from trees. These acts signified great honor to Jesus by the multitudes.

Their words acclaimed Jesus as the Son of David. They were quoting from Psalm 118:25, 26, a hymn used by people going to worship in the temple. "Hosanna" meant "God, save us." However, by the first century, "Hosanna" had become a word used in praising God. Two of the titles in Psalm 118:25, 26 were titles for the Messiah. Of course, Son of David meant the descendant of David sent by God to fulfill divine promises of an everlasting kingdom ruled by one of David's descendants (2 Sam. 7:12–17). "He that cometh" was also at times used as a title for the One who was to come (see Matt. 11:3). Unfortunately, the actions of the people that day and later in the week showed that they welcomed Jesus as the kind of Messiah they wanted, not the kind of King He had come to be.

3. Created a great stir (vv. 10, 11)

> 10 And when he was come into Jerusalem, all the city was moved, saying, Who is this?
>
> 11 And the multitude said, This is Jesus the prophet of Nazareth of Galilee.

The word *moved* is too mild to describe the great stir of excitement in Jerusalem. The word was used in Matthew 27:51 to describe an earthquake. The whole city was asking, "Who is this?" The crowds answered this question by referring to Jesus as "the prophet of Nazareth of Galilee." Why didn't they acclaim Him as Son of David?

Perhaps they were thinking of Moses' promise of a prophet and thus intended "prophet" to mean Messiah. If not, perhaps they were merely being cautious. After all, even Jesus had cautioned people about publicly declaring Him as Messiah. Many of the people of Judea knew that Micah 5:2 predicted that the Messiah would come from David's native city Bethlehem in his home area of Judah, not from an obscure village in distant Galilee (John 7:40, 41).

II. Cleansing the Temple (Matt. 21:12–17)

1. Attacked the money-makers (v. 12)

> 12 And Jesus went into the temple of God, and cast out all them that sold and bought in the temple, and overthrew the

tables of the moneychangers, and the seats of them that sold doves.

Jews who came to worship in the temple needed animals to offer as sacrifices. The poorer people were allowed to bring doves. Many worshipers traveled great distances to come to Jerusalem, and the animals had to be declared unblemished by the priests. These two factors suggested a marketing opportunity for people always looking for new ways to make money. The temple authorities, who were always looking for ways to enrich themselves, also saw this opportunity. Thus, booths were set up in the court of the Gentiles where travelers could buy sacrificial animals guaranteed to pass inspection by the priests. No doubt, the chief priests, who ran the temple, received a percentage of this lucrative enterprise.

Jews also needed Jewish coins with which to pay the temple tax. Foreign coins, which were in wide circulation, often had heads of Roman emperors on them or some insignia that suggested paganism. Therefore, tables were set up where a Jew could exchange foreign money for Jewish money.

The sellers of animals and the exchangers of money thus justified their work as a service to worshipers. They justified their presence in the temple's outer court as a convenience for these same worshipers. Yet Jesus apparently didn't accept these as legitimate enterprises in the temple, even in the large outer court. When Jesus entered the temple, He acted anything but meekly, at least in the usual sense of our word *meek*. He boldly turned over the tables and the seats of those who made money in the temple. Matthew also says that He drove them out.

2. Condemned making the temple into a den of thieves (v. 13)

13 And said unto them, It is written, My house shall be called the house of prayer; but ye have made it a den of thieves.

Jesus explained His actions by quoting Isaiah 56:7 and Jeremiah 7:11. Mark 11:17 quotes all of Isaiah 56:7, including the words "for all nations." God's purpose all along has been to provide a way for all people—Gentiles as well as Jews—to worship Him. Under the old covenant, one sign of this was the provision in the Jewish temple for a place where Gentiles could worship. Although Gentiles could not enter the courts where Jews brought their animals to the priests, Gentiles were supposed to be able to pray in the court of the Gentiles. Those who made money had perverted the divine purpose of the court of the Gentiles from a place of prayer to a place of business.

Jeremiah 7:11 was part of the outspoken prophet's famous temple sermon. He condemned the hypocrites of his day for living in sin and coming to the temple to worship. Jeremiah compared them to thieves, who ventured forth to commit crimes and then retreated to a secret den. Jesus' use of Jeremiah 7:11 condemned the hypocrisy of those who used the temple for their own profit, and His use of "thieves" shows that the money-makers were robbing the people. The animal sellers sold animals for more than they were worth and the money changers charged an unfair fee for their services.

By cleansing the temple, Jesus showed not only the boldness of a prophet but also the authority of One who looked on the temple as His Father's house. Jesus in essence was claiming to have authority over the temple, an ultimate authority that dared to condemn the priestly authorities who ran the temple.

This bold action in the temple was a key factor that led to His death. The ruling Jewish religious court, the Sanhedrin, was presided over by the high priest, who also happened to administer the temple. On the Sanhedrin were both Pharisees and Sadducees. For a long time, the Pharisees had hated Jesus, because He defied their legalistic traditions. By invading the domain of the Sadducees, the temple, Jesus aroused their fury. Thus, these two groups, who seldom agreed on anything, decided to get rid of Jesus (Mark 11:18).

3. Aroused the anger of the chief priests (vv. 14–17)

Jesus showed His authority over the temple also by healing people there (v. 14). The scribes (Pharisees) and chief priests (Sadducees) had watched all these things, apparently including the royal entry. They were angry because even children were caught up in praising Jesus (v. 15). Jesus responded to their anger by quoting Psalm 8:2 (v. 16). Then Jesus left Jerusalem and went to the nearby village of Bethany, where he was staying (v. 17).

PRONUNCIATION GUIDE

| Bethphage | [BETH fayge] |
| Sanhedrin | [san HE drihn] |

SUMMARY OF BIBLE TRUTHS

1. Jesus was a Servant-King, who saves by humble self-giving.
2. Jesus' purpose in the royal entry was to emphasize this truth.
3. The people wanted a powerful earthly king.
4. Jesus condemned those who perverted God's purpose for the temple.
5. By cleansing the temple, Jesus claimed authority over the temple.
6. Jesus was meek in the sense of being humble, not in the sense of not showing righteous indignation and holy boldness.

APPLYING THE BIBLE

1. Lasting peace. Had Jesus come as the conquering Messiah-King, our ultimate response to him would be one of resentment. In a speech delivered to the U.S. Senate, President Woodrow Wilson stated that peace must be "without victory.... Victory would mean peace forced upon the loser, a victor's terms imposed upon the vanquished. It would be accepted in humiliation, under duress, at an intolerable sacrifice, and would leave a sting, a resentment, a bitter memory upon which terms of peace would rest, not permanently, but only as upon quicksand. Only a peace between equals can last."[1]

The wisdom of God made it happen. Jesus emptied Himself and took on the form of a servant (our equal) and made available a peace with no resentment. It seems like a strange way to save a world, but in riding to Jerusalem on a donkey, He did just that.

2. The meekness of Jesus. General George S. Patton said, "Wars may be fought with weapons, but they are won by men. It is the spirit of the men who follow and of the man who leads that gains the victory." Entering Jerusalem on the back of a donkey demonstrated the spirit and character of Jesus. The battle for redemption was won because of who He is.

3. Creating a great stir. When Jesus entered Jerusalem, it created a great stir. At Passover, people were hoping that God would send the Messiah. People were looking for a hero. People are still looking for heroes today, and in many ways we look for them in the same arenas as the people in Jesus' day.

Sixty percent of children ages 9-13 say they have a hero. The top five categories for their heroes are:
- relatives/friends (52.9%),
- athletes (31.5%),
- religious figures (11.3%),
- fictional characters (11.3%), and
- political/historical figures (8.7%)[2]

Religious leaders and fictional characters tie for influence, and their numbers combined still fall short of the influence held by sports heroes. Convincing people that spiritual things matter is the continuing challenge facing the church.

4. Cleansing the temple. Among several business principles held by Japanese businessman Konosuke Matsushita,[3] the following illustrate a strong commitment to business ethics.
- Treat the people you do business with as if they were part of your family.
- After-sales service is more important than assistance before sales.
- Don't sell customers goods they are attracted to; sell them goods that will benefit them.

The righteous indignation demonstrated by Jesus in cleansing the temple of the money changers may be due in part to the fact that each of these principles was violated. There were no ethics involved at all. The trade benefited the money changers and the religious leaders who received a kickback. There was no concern for the individual, no familial consideration, no service, and certainly nothing with their best interest in mind. It broke the heart of Jesus to see such abuse in a place that was intended for prayer.

5. Never an acceptable way to do a bad thing. An airline worker was convicted of stealing 100,000 cards from the mail he was loading on airplanes. He looked for envelopes that might contain cash or checks and over a three-year period may have helped himself to as much as $500,000. After pleading guilty, his attorney told news reporters that he took the money to play the lottery, hoping to pay expenses for two disabled children. His case reminds us that there is never an acceptable way to do a bad thing. The money changers in the temple were doing a bad thing. They were taking advantage of the poorest of the poor and making a profit in the process.

6. We need a house of prayer. The names of the towns in this study are significant. They further illustrate the reasons Jesus reacted with such anger in the temple at the sight of the money changers. Bethphage (Matt. 21:1), where today's lesson begins, means "house of the unripened fruit" while Bethany (Matt. 21:17), where today's lesson ends, means "house of misery." Jesus knew that between the bitterness of life (unripened fruit) and the pressures of life (misery) people needed a house of prayer. Life continues to be bitter and difficult for people today. Our churches need to be houses of prayer—not contention. How do you think people view your church today?

TEACHING THE BIBLE

- *Main Idea:* Jesus' royal entry into Jerusalem declared that He was a humble Servant-King.
- *Suggested Teaching Aim:* To lead adults to accept Jesus as a humble Servant-King and not try to force Him into the role of political king.

A TEACHING OUTLINE

1. Royal Entry into Jerusalem (Matt. 21:1–11)
2. Cleansing the Temple (Matt. 21:12–17)

Introduce the Bible Study

Use number 2, "The Meekness of Jesus," in "Applying the Bible" to introduce the lesson.

Search for Biblical Truth

Be sure every member has a Bible. You might have some extra ones available so all can participate in the Scripture search. Ask members to open their Bibles to Matthew 21:1–17. Locate Jerusalem and the possible location of Bethphage on a map of Jesus' ministry. Ask members who have reference Bibles to locate the Old Testament Scriptures referred to in verses 4, 5 (Zech. 9:9 and Isa. 62:11). Ask another member to look up Matthew 11:29 and find one word Jesus used to describe Himself that is similar to a word used in Zechariah. (Meek, lowly.) Using the material in "Studying the Bible," point out how Jesus' entrance emphasized His humbleness and not His political ambitions.

DISCUSS: If Jesus had asked you how He could have entered Jerusalem to communicate that He was a humble Servant-King, what would you have responded? What dangers did Jesus face if the people misunderstood?

Ask members to find two titles in Matthew 21:9 that the people applied to Jesus that indicated they believed Jesus to be the Messiah. ("Son of David" and "He that cometh in the name of the Lord.")

Use "Studying the Bible" to explain how the Jews expected the Messiah to come at Passover. Ask members to turn to Psalm 118:25–26 to find the psalm from which the people quoted their praise. Point out that the people sang this psalm as they went to worship in the temple. Ask, What kind of Messiah do you think the people expected?

DISCUSS: How have we forced Jesus to be the kind of Savior we want Him to be instead of the kind of Savior He really is? What can we do to keep this from happening again?

Ask half the members to look at Matthew 21:10 and the other half to turn to Matthew 27:51. Ask each group to find a word in their verse that describes how the city of Jerusalem was affected ("moved" and "quaked"). Point out that the Greek word is the same in both places. Ask, If you had been a reporter writing about Jesus' entry into Jerusalem, what headline would you have used?

Ask members to look at Matthew 21:12. Ask, What was the first thing Jesus did when He entered Jerusalem? What do you think the people expected Him to do? How do you think this made the people feel when He cleansed the temple instead of setting Himself up as king?

Explain why the Jews had set up shop to provide animals and coinage in the court of the Gentiles. Ask, Why do you think Jesus drove the shopkeepers out?
1. The traders were taking advantage of the people who traveled great distances to worship God.
2. The business interfered with the Gentiles' place of worship.
3. The traders were cheating the people by charging great prices to exchange coins and to buy "approved" sacrificial animals.

Give the Truth a Personal Focus

Read the six "Summary of Bible Truths" statements. Distribute paper and pencils. Ask members to think about ways they have tried to force Jesus to be the kind of Lord they want instead of allowing Him to be who He is. Close in prayer that all will accept Jesus as a humble Servant-King and not try to force Him into any other role.

---

1. Woodrow Wilson, Address to the Senate, Jan. 22, 1917.
2. "Sports Illustrated for Kids," cited in *USA Today,* March 4, 1995.
3. Cindy Kano, *Fortune,* March 31, 1997, 107.

February 13, 2000

Watching for Christ's Return

Background Passage: Matthew 24:1–25:13
Focal Passage: Matthew 24:45–25:13

Matthew 24–25 focuses on Jesus' teachings about the future. These chapters provide the foundation for some basic Christian beliefs. The basic teachings are: (1) Christ's coming is certain, but the time is uncertain, and (2) people demonstrate their belief in this teaching by being ready for His coming. These chapters also contain some points on which Christians do not agree.

▶**Study Aim:** To explain what Jesus taught about watching for His return.

STUDYING THE BIBLE

OUTLINE AND SUMMARY

I. Questions About the Future (Matt. 24:1–3)
II. Events Prior to the End (Matt. 24:4–28)
   1. The end is not yet (24:4–14)
   2. The abomination of desolation (24:15–28)
III. Christ's Future Coming (Matt. 24:29–41)
   1. Certainty of His coming (24:29–35)
   2. Uncertainty of the time (24:36–41)
IV. Call to Watch (Matt. 24:42–25:13)
   1. A faithful and wise servant (24:42–47)
   2. An evil servant (24:48–51)
   3. Wise and foolish virgins (25:1–5)
   4. Judgment on the unprepared (25:6–13)

The disciples asked Jesus about the time of the destruction of the temple and of His return (24:1–3). Jesus warned against assuming that every time of trouble meant that the end had come (24:4–14). He spoke of the abomination of desolation and a time of troubles (24:15–28). He spoke of the certainty of His return (24:29–35) but the uncertainty of the time (24:36–41). He illustrated His call for watchfulness by telling of a faithful and wise servant (24:42–47). He illustrated what not to do by telling of an evil servant (24:48–51). Jesus told the parable of the wise and foolish virgins (25:1–5). The wise ones got ready, but the foolish ones were excluded because they did not prepare (25:6–13).

I. Questions About the Future (Matt. 24:1–3)

After the disciples spoke of the impressive buildings of the temple, Jesus predicted the destruction of the temple (24:1, 2). The disciples asked Jesus about the time when the temple would be destroyed and about His future coming (24:3).

II. Events Prior to the End (Matt. 24:4–28)
1. The end is not yet (24:4–14)
Jesus warned them not to assume that every disaster meant that the end had arrived. False messiahs (24:4, 5); wars and natural disasters (24:6, 7); persecution and betrayal (24:9, 10); false prophets, great evil, and apostasy (24:11, 12) are only the beginning of troubles to be expected by believers (24:8). During those times Christians are to remain faithful and take the good news to all nations (24:13, 14).

2. The abomination of desolation (24:15–28)
Many Bible students think these verses are Jesus' answer to the question about the fall of Jerusalem and the destruction of the temple, although these events foreshadow events related to Christ's coming (24:15). The instructions given in verses 16–20 were obeyed by Christians when they saw the Roman armies surround Jerusalem (see Luke 21:20–24). Some Bible students interpret verses 21 through 26 as a final great tribulation, and others see these verses describing troubles over a longer period of time. Verses 27 and 28 make clear that Christ's coming will be as visible as lightning.

III. Christ's Future Coming (Matt. 24:29–41)
1. Certainty of His coming (24:29–35)
The real but cataclysmic events of Christ's coming are summarized in verses 29 through 31. Verses 32 through 35 stress the nearness of Christ's coming.

2. Uncertainty of the time (24:36–41)
No one but God knows the time of Christ's coming (24:36). As in the time of Noah, people will be going about their usual tasks and will be caught unprepared for Christ's coming (24:37–39). A separation of people will take place, depending on their readiness for Christ's coming (24:40, 41).

IV. Call to Watch (Matt. 24:42–25:13)
1. A faithful and wise servant (24:42–47)

> **45 Who then is a faithful and wise servant, whom his lord hath made ruler over his household, to give them meat in due season?**
>
> **46 Blessed is that servant, whom his lord when he cometh shall find so doing.**
>
> **47 Verily I say unto you, That he shall make him ruler over all his goods.**

Because no one knows when Christ will return, each should watch (24:42). Christ's coming will be like a thief in the night in that many will not be expecting Him at that time (24:43). Therefore, each person should be ready at all times (24:44). Two words describe one who is ready: *faithful* and *wise*. The word *servant* translates the Greek word for "slave." This particular slave was a steward or manager whom an owner left in charge of his household. Among his duties was to feed the other slaves.

February 13, 2000

A wise manager listens to the owner's instructions, and a faithful manager obeys what the owner said to do. Because the owner might return at any time, the only way to be ready is to follow his instructions. Therefore, when the owner returns unexpectedly, he will find the manager carrying out his orders. The owner will promote the manager as a reward.

2. An evil servant (24:48–51)

> **48 But and if that evil servant shall say in his heart, My lord delayeth his coming;**
>
> **49 And shall begin to smite his fellow-servants, and to eat and drink with the drunken;**
>
> **50 The lord of that servant shall come in a day when he looketh not for him, and in an hour that he is not aware of,**
>
> **51 And shall cut him asunder, and appoint him his portion with the hypocrites: there shall be weeping and gnashing of teeth.**

This servant had the same job as the one in verses 45 through 47; however, he was not just neglectful; he was evil. He not only did not care for the other slaves, but also he misused his authority to beat them. And he misused his position to get drunk.

These evil actions stemmed from the evil slave's attitude about the master and his warning that he might return at any time. When the master did not return right away, the evil slave noted that he was delaying his coming. He must have decided that he would continue to delay his return; perhaps he thought that the master would not return at all. At any rate, he used the master's delay as an opportunity to do as he pleased. His true nature came to the surface. He disobeyed the master's orders; he mistreated his fellow slaves; and he abused his own body with excessive drink.

One day—when the slave-manager least expected him to return—the master showed up. The master's unexpected arrival gave the manager no time to try to hide his sins. He was caught in the act. As punishment, the master cut him to pieces. The last part of verse 51 reflects the Lord's punishment of those who use the Lord's absence to do evil.

3. Wise and foolish virgins (25:1–5)

> **1 Then shall the kingdom of heaven be likened unto ten virgins, which took their lamps, and went forth to meet the bridegroom.**
>
> **2 And five of them were wise, and five were foolish.**
>
> **3 They that were foolish took their lamps, and took no oil with them:**
>
> **4 But the wise took oil in their vessels with their lamps.**
>
> **5 While the bridegroom tarried, they all slumbered and slept.**

Like the parable in Matthew 20:1–16, the parable in Matthew 25:1–13 used a typical situation from life to illustrate realities about human relations with God. The former parable was about a landowner hiring workers for his harvest; the latter was about a wedding. Although

February 13 2000

the situations were familiar to Jesus' hearers, Jesus depicted some of the characters acting in ways different from the way people normally acted in such situations.

This parable focuses on ten virgins. The word *virgin* is used here to describe what we would call "bridesmaids." These were young women, who were probably friends of the bride (who is never mentioned in the story). According to the wedding customs of that time, the groom and a procession went to the bride's house, where she and her bridesmaids joined the procession to go to the groom's house for the wedding and banquet.

The bridesmaids' part in the procession was to have lamps and oil to provide illumination as the wedding party made its way through the unlighted streets. The word *lamps* referred to oil lamps, which were lighted, hoisted on poles, and used for light.

All the bridesmaids had their lamps, but only five had brought the oil necessary to make the lamps burn. This was the one fact that initially distinguished the wise from the foolish virgins. We are not told why five did not bring oil. Jesus' hearers could not imagine any bridesmaid being so foolish. That was exactly Jesus' point. This part of the parable reflects how people react toward the certainty of the Lord's coming and the uncertainty of the time of His coming. No bridesmaid would be so foolish as to risk not being ready to join the wedding party, but many people are foolish enough not to prepare for the much more important procession of the Lord to the marriage feast of the Lamb.

For some unexplained reason, the groom was late. This had been known to happen, but it was not normal. Jesus was illustrating the fact that many people consider His delayed coming an excuse for not being ready when He does come.

4. Judgment on the unprepared (25:6–13)

> **6 And at midnight there was a cry made, Behold, the bridegroom cometh; go ye out to meet him.**
>
> **7 Then all those virgins arose, and trimmed their lamps.**
>
> **8 And the foolish said unto the wise, Give us of your oil; for our lamps are gone out.**
>
> **9 But the wise answered, saying, Not so; lest there be not enough for us and you: but go ye rather to them that sell, and buy for yourselves.**
>
> **10 And while they went to buy, the bridegroom came; and they that were ready went in with him to the marriage: and the door was shut.**
>
> **11 Afterward came also the other virgins, saying, Lord, Lord, open to us.**
>
> **12 But he answered and said, Verily I say unto you, I know you not.**
>
> **13 Watch therefore, for ye know neither the day nor the hour wherein the Son of man cometh.**

The folly of the five unprepared bridesmaids became apparent when they were awakened by the cry that the groom was near. All ten were asleep. The wise could sleep because they were ready. The ones without

February 13, 2000

oil should have been taking advantage of this last opportunity to purchase oil. Only after the groom arrived did they recognize their plight. The wise bridesmaids were not being selfish but practical in refusing to share their oil. They did not have enough for all ten to perform their functions.

The refusal of the groom to let the foolish girls in was probably not something true to life, but it illustrates the seriousness of not being ready when the Lord returns. It will be too late then to get ready. The foolish people who postponed getting ready for His coming will be left outside the door to the kingdom. Their fate will be sealed by their own foolish failure to get ready.

The word *watch* can mean "stay awake" (Matt. 26:38, 40, 41); but, in this passage, it has the more general meaning of "be ready" (24:44). The wise virgins were ready for the groom whenever he came; the foolish ones were not ready no matter when he came.

SUMMARY OF BIBLE TRUTHS

1. Because the time of Christ's return is unknown, people should be ready at any time.
2. "Watch" means "be ready" for the Lord's return.
3. Wise people prepare; foolish people don't.
4. Faithful servants of Christ will share in His glory.
5. Evil people and people who failed to get ready will be excluded.

APPLYING THE BIBLE

1. The importance of staying awake. Did you hear about the thief who fell asleep in a home he was burglarizing? A woman came home in the early morning hours and found her front door ajar, a window broken, and jewelry boxes emptied. She also found the intruder snoring at the foot of her bed.

The woman quietly made her way downstairs to call police, who arrived moments later to awaken and arrest the sleeping man. Jesus told the story of the ten virgins to emphasize the importance of being prepared and being alert to His coming. A church that fails to be alert is like a thief falling asleep. Neither is very effective in fulfilling their mission.

2. Seduction. G. Campbell Morgan said the great danger in our careless waiting would be "the seduction of a false Christ."[1] Growing cult activity in our day gives credibility to Morgan's warning. So does the growing attraction to secular idols that have found their way into the heart of mankind.

3. Looking for signs. The thirteen-year cicada bug made its appearance in the spring of 1998, the same year that the "blame it all on El Nino" weather pattern made its way into every arena of our lives. Some saw these events as cataclysmic parts of a prophetic event. Others saw them as natural events that just happened to occur in the same year. The Christian is encouraged to exercise discernment when looking at events that make their way into our lives.

4. No man knows the hour. In 1988 Edgar C. Wisenant published a book entitled *88 Reasons Why the Rapture Will Be in 1988*. Obviously,

February 13 2000

it didn't happen. I doubt anyone really expected it to, except maybe the author. Jesus said no one knows the day or the hour.

5. Common responses to difficult times. Warren Wiersbe[2] offers an encouraging application to the text for this lesson. Difficult days are inevitable. All believers will face trying times sooner or later as we await the second coming of Christ. The following five statements apply today's lesson to the heart of every believer:

- **Don't be deceived** (Matt. 24:4, 11). False prophets and teachers will arise, but we know the truth.
- **Don't be discouraged** (Matt. 24:6). Bad things happen, but God is still on the throne.
- **Don't be defeated** (Matt. 24:13). At times it may seem pointless, but our witness still matters.
- **Don't be doubtful** (Matt. 24:34, 35). Things change and disappointments happen, but God's word abides forever.
- **Don't be distracted** (Matt. 24:42). Everything vies for your attention, but we are watching and working until He comes.

6. What if it were today? Hymn texts can challenge us at a deeper level than mere words. "What If It Were Today" asks a haunting question:

> Faithful and true would He find us here
> If He should come today?
> Watching in gladness and not in fear,
> If He should come today?
> Signs of His coming multiply,
> Morning light breaks in eastern sky,
> Watch, for the time is drawing nigh,
> What if it were today?
> —Leila Naylor Morris

TEACHING THE BIBLE

- *Main Idea:* Jesus warns us to be ready at any moment for His return.
- *Suggested Teaching Aim:* To lead adults to identify what they can do to prepare for Jesus' return.

A TEACHING OUTLINE

1. *Questions About the Future (Matt. 24:1–3)*
2. *Events Prior to the End (Matt. 24:4–28)*
3. *Christ's Future Coming (Matt. 24:29–41)*
4. *Call to Watch (Matt. 24:42—25:13)*

Introduce the Bible Study

Use number 1, "The Importance of Staying Awake," in "Applying the Bible" to introduce the lesson. Point out that Jesus urged His followers to watch for His return.

Search for Biblical Truth

IN ADVANCE, enlist someone to present as a monologue by Jesus the information in the summary statements in "Outline and Summary." Begin by saying: "One day My disciples asked Me about the destruction of the temple and My return. This is what I told them. 'Don't assume that every time of trouble means that the end has come.'" Put each of the statements into a word of warning from Jesus and read this to the class to overview the Scripture.

Using the material in "Studying the Bible," lecture briefly covering points I and II in the outline on the previous page. (These verses set the context for the lesson.)

Organize the class into two groups and give each group one of the assignments. Allow six to seven minutes for study and then call for reports.

1. Based on Matthew 24:42–51:
- What two words describe one who is ready?
- Compare and contrast the faithful and wise servant with the evil servant.
- How are we like these two servants? How are we different?

2. Based on Matthew 25:1–13:
- Who are the main characters in this parable?
- Describe the wedding situation Jesus portrayed.
- Why were the five wise bridesmaids justified in not sharing their oil?
- How are we like the five wise bridesmaids? the five foolish bridesmaids?

Give the Truth a Personal Focus

IN ADVANCE, on a chalkboard or a large sheet of paper, write these statements. (Italicized words are the words that need to be changed and are for your convenience; do not italicize them when you write them out.) Ask members to change a word or words in each sentence to make it a true statement.
- Because the time of Christ's return is *known,* people should be ready at any time.
- "Watch" means "be ready" for the *devil's* return.
- *Foolish* people prepare; *wise* people don't.
- *Indifferent* servants of Christ will share in His glory.
- Evil people and people who failed to get ready will be *included.*

Ask, What do you need to do to be ready for Christ's return? (If you have unsaved members present, encourage any who need to accept Christ to talk with you after the class.) Challenge believers to live in such a way that they would not be embarrassed if Christ caught them at any point in their lives.

---

1. G. Campbell Morgan, *Life Applications from Every Chapter in the Bible* (Grand Rapids: Revell, 1994), 307.
2. Warren Wiersbe, *With the Word* (Nashville: Thomas Nelson Publishers, 1982), 650.

Death of Jesus

February 20 2000

Background Passage: Matthew 27:32–61
Focal Passage: Matthew 27:38–54

The death and resurrection of Jesus are the heart of the good news (1 Cor. 15:3, 4). All four Gospels make these the climactic events of Jesus' life and ministry. The account of the death of Jesus in Matthew's Gospel is a series of brief looks at the people around the cross, with Jesus Himself as the focal point.

▶**Study Aim:** *To describe what the people at the cross said and did.*

STUDYING THE BIBLE

OUTLINE AND SUMMARY
I. Crucifixion of Jesus (Matt. 27:32–50)
   1. Those who crucified Him (27:32–37)
   2. Those who mocked Him (27:38–44)
   3. Jesus' cry from the cross (27:45–50)
II. Events Following Jesus' Death (Matt. 27:51–61)
   1. Miracles (27:51–53)
   2. Centurion's confession (27: 54)
   3. Women's watch (27:55, 56)
   4. Burial of Jesus (27:57–61)

The soldiers who crucified Jesus cast lots for His clothes (vv. 32–37). The passersby, the religious leaders, and the two thieves mocked Jesus (vv. 38–44). During Jesus' suffering, He cried out in the words of Psalm 22:1 (vv. 45–50). When Jesus died, the temple veil was torn, an earthquake occurred, and dead believers were raised up (vv. 51–53). The Roman centurion confessed Jesus as Son of God (v. 54). Three women followers were watching (vv. 55, 56). Joseph of Arimathea placed Jesus' body in his own tomb (vv. 57–61).

I. Crucifixion of Jesus (Matt. 27:32–50)
1. Those who crucified Him (vv. 32–37)
Because Jesus was unable to carry the cross, the soldiers conscripted Simon of Cyrene (v. 32). When they arrived at Golgotha, Jesus refused the drugged wine which was offered to Him by the soldiers (vv. 33, 34). The soldiers cast lots for Jesus' clothes (vv. 35, 36). Over the cross of Jesus was the accusation against Jesus, "THIS IS JESUS THE KING OF THE JEWS" (v. 37).

2. Those who mocked Him (vv. 38–44)
> 38 Then were there two thieves crucified with him, one on the right hand, and another on the left.

The word *thieves* can mean what our word means, or it can refer to rebels against Rome, who stole as part of their terrorism. Whatever their

February 20, 2000

crime, these two men were sinners and criminals. The fact that Jesus died with sinners points to the purpose of the cross—Jesus died for sinners.

> **39 And they that passed by reviled him, wagging their heads,**
>
> **40 And saying, Thou that destroyest the temple, and buildest it in three days, save thyself. If thou be the Son of God, come down from the cross.**

The crowds who passed by insulted (blasphemed) Jesus. They taunted Him to save Himself. They knew about the false accusations made at His trial. Jesus was accused of saying that He would tear down the temple building and rebuild it in three days (Matt. 26:61; see John 2:19–22).

The passersby used the same clause that Satan had used in the wilderness temptations (Matt. 4:3). They taunted Jesus, "Since you are the Son of God, save yourself." This had been a recurring temptation for Jesus. Satan tempted Him again on the cross to use His power to save Himself. Jesus could have saved Himself. When Jesus was arrested, He said that He could have summoned twelve legions of angels to rescue Him (Matt. 26:53, 54). Instead, He voluntarily gave Himself into the hands of those who intended to crucify Him.

> **41 Likewise also the chief priests mocking him, with the scribes and elders, said,**
>
> **42 He saved others; himself he cannot save. If he be the King of the Israel, let him now come down from the cross, and we will believe him.**
>
> **43 He trusted in God; let him deliver him now, if he will have him: for he said, I am the Son of God.**
>
> **44 The thieves also, which were crucified with him, cast the same in his teeth.**

The chief priests also mocked (made fun of) Jesus, being joined by the scribes and elders—the groups that conspired to condemn Jesus (Matt. 26:3, 57; 27:1). They taunted Him by saying that Jesus claimed to have saved others, but He was unable to save Himself. Their intended mockery contained more truth than they realized. Jesus could have saved Himself from the cross; but He knew that if He saved Himself, He would be unable to save sinners.

They also taunted Jesus about His professed trust in God, whom He claimed was His Father. The religious leaders made fun of this man who claimed to be the Son of God. He trusted God, but where was God, that He allowed His Son to die in this terrible way? Even the two dying criminals echoed the words of the other mocking voices.

3. Jesus' cry from the cross (vv. 45–50)

> **45 Now from the sixth hour there was darkness over all the land unto the ninth hour.**
>
> **46 And about the ninth hour Jesus cried with a loud voice, saying, Eli, Eli, lama sabachthani? that is to say, My God, my God, why hast thou forsaken me?**

47 Some of them that stood there, when they heard that, said, This man calleth for Elias.

48 And straightway one of them ran, and took a spunge, and filled it with vinegar, and put it on a reed, and gave him to drink.

49 The rest said, Let be, let us see whether Elias will come to save him.

50 Jesus, when he had cried again with a loud voice, yielded up the ghost.

Jesus was crucified at the third hour of the Jewish day, or about 9:00 A.M. (Mark 15:25). At the sixth hour (noon) darkness spread over the land until the ninth hour (3:00 P.M.). Toward the end of the three hours of darkness, Jesus cried out in words that some misunderstood. Others knew Aramaic and were near enough to recognize His cry as the words of Psalm 22:1. The psalmist's sense of being forsaken by God was echoed in the cry of Jesus from the cross. His cry was a cry and a prayer. When the crucifixion accounts of all four Gospels are compared, we find seven sayings of Jesus from the cross (Luke 23:34, 43, 46; John 19:27, 28, 30).

Preachers, scholars, and every sincere believer stand in awe before Jesus' cry, "My God, my God, why hast thou forsaken me?" We do our best to understand and explain the cry, but all our efforts fall short of unlocking the full mystery of Christ's atoning death or of beginning to fathom the depths of what He suffered for us.

Being crucified was a painful, humiliating way to die; but the New Testament does not dwell on the horrors of being crucified. Instead it presents us with the Son of God enduring the worst of all sufferings—a sense of being forsaken by God. Sin separates from God; and somehow as Jesus died, God "made him to be sin for us, who knew no sin; that we might be made the righteousness of God in him" (2 Cor. 5:21). Yet we also must remember "that God was in Christ, reconciling the world unto himself" (2 Cor. 5:19); and that the cross reveals not only the love of Jesus but the love of God (Rom. 5:6–8).

II. Events Following Jesus' Death (Matt. 27:51–61)

1. Miracles (vv. 51–53)

51 And, behold, the veil of the temple was rent in twain from the top to the bottom; and the earth did quake, and the rocks rent;

52 And the graves were opened; and many bodies of the saints which slept arose,

53 And came out of the graves after his resurrection, and went into the holy city, and appeared unto many.

Just as the birth of Jesus was announced by miraculous signs, so was His death. In addition to the miraculous darkness of His final three hours of suffering, Matthew mentions three other miracles: the temple veil, the earthquake, and resurrections.

February 20, 2000

The veil refers to the veil that closed off the holy of holies, which represented the presence of God, from the rest of the temple. Only the high priest could enter and he only once a year with the proper sacrifices for himself and for the people's sins. When Jesus died, that veil was torn from top to bottom—as if by the hand of God. This signified that God had opened access to Himself for all sinners through the sacrifice of Jesus Christ, who is also our great High Priest. The Book of Hebrews emphasizes Christ as our priest and sacrifice. As a result, the inspired writer says, "Let us therefore come boldly unto the throne of grace, that we may obtain mercy, and find grace to help in time of need" (Heb. 4:16).

Later Jewish sources mention an earthquake about forty years prior to the fall of Jerusalem in A.D. 70. This may have been the earthquake mentioned in Matthew 27:51.

At the same time, many graves were opened—perhaps by the earthquake. Later after Jesus had been raised from the dead, the resurrected bodies of dead believers appeared to many people. Apparently these were the dead people of faith of Old Testament times. This miracle shows that the Old Testament believers would share in the new covenant salvation.

2. Centurion's confession (v. 54)

54 Now when the centurion, and they that were with him, watching Jesus, saw the earthquake, and those things that were done, they feared greatly, saying, Truly this was the Son of God.

A centurion was an officer in the Roman army who commanded one hundred men. This particular centurion was apparently in command of the soldiers who crucified Jesus. He and his soldiers had been near enough to the cross to see and hear what took place.

His response when Jesus died is remarkable. Some translators and interpreters think that the centurion's words indicate a good man who was right to trust God as Father (see Luke 23:47). However, others are convinced that the centurion confessed Jesus as the Son of God. When others at the cross were mocking the dying Jesus, the pagan Roman army officer confessed Jesus as the Son of God.

With the exception of a few faithful women and one of the Twelve, even the close friends of Jesus chose not to come to the crucifixion. They considered it the end of their hopes and dreams for Jesus as Messiah, and they feared that the enemies of Jesus would soon be looking for them. Yet at that time, two people believed at the cross—the penitent thief and the Roman centurion. In a way, they were comparable to the first groups to seek the newborn Jesus—outcast shepherds and pagan wise men. The centurion's confession foreshadowed the millions of Gentiles who eventually would acclaim Jesus as the Son of God.

3. Women's watch (vv. 55, 56)

Matthew did not mention any of the male disciples being there, including himself. John's Gospel mentions the beloved disciple. However, some loyal women watched with sorrow as Jesus was crucified:

Mary Magdalene, Mary the mother of James and Joses, and the mother of Zebedee's children (James and John).

4. Burial of Jesus (vv. 57–61)

Joseph of Arimathea asked Pilate for permission to take the body of Jesus, and Pilate issued the order (vv. 57, 58). After wrapping the body in a clean linen cloth, Joseph laid the body in his own new tomb, which had been hewn out of rock. Then he rolled a great stone across the tomb's door (vv. 59, 60). Mary Magdalene and the other Mary were sitting near the tomb (v. 61).

PRONUNCIATION GUIDE

Arimathea	[ahr ih muh THEE uh]
Cyrene	[sigh REE nee]
Lama	[LAH muh]
Sabachthani	[sah BAHK thu nigh]
Zebedee	[ZEB uh dee]

SUMMARY OF BIBLE TRUTHS

1. Jesus died with sinners and for sinners.
2. He voluntarily chose to give Himself in order to save others.
3. Jesus endured the suffering of one separated from God.
4. Some people reject Jesus and His death for them.
5. Other people confess Jesus as Son of God and Savior.

APPLYING THE BIBLE

1. True confession. "Psychoanalysis is the probing of mind by mind; confession is the communion of conscience and God" (Fulton J. Sheen).

2. Two kinds of people. "There are only two sorts of men: the one the just, who believe themselves sinners; the other sinners, who believe themselves just" (Blaise Pascal).

3. Substitute. When you write the word *substitute,* you are spelling a one-word sermon on the theology of salvation. There are three "t's" in the word just as there were three crosses on Golgotha the day Jesus was crucified. The middle "t" is the cross of Christ because there is a place for both "u" and "I" beside it. When Christ died, He took the place that belonged to you and me. He became the sin substitute for us.

4. People like us. "God was executed by people painfully like us, in a society very similar to our own . . . by a corrupt church, a timid politician, and a fickle proletariat led by professional agitators."[1]

5. It is finished. In a sermon titled *It is Finished* by Wayne Brouwer, we are invited to see how different people understood the words of Jesus as He hung dying on the cross.

- For Judas, the words indicated betrayal complete, blood money gone, business taken care of.
- For Peter, his denial meant he would never be able to go home again, not even to Galilee. He would never be able to show his face in public. He was ruined. It is finished.

February 20 2000

February 20, 2000

- Pilate endured a political pressure point, faced another sleepless night with a wife who heard voices, washed his hands again, and watched from the portico of his palace and with a sigh of relief whispered, "It is finished."
- An unrepentant thief said, "You're done for, and so am I. Here we go."
- A broken-hearted thief heard the words "It is finished" and discovered that his past had disappeared. He felt like a newborn baby. With Simeon he could say, "Now, Lord, let me die in peace. My eyes have seen your salvation. It is finished."
- The centurion looked up at Jesus and shook his head. It's finished now, but something good died today—something that I once believed in—justice. We're the worse for it. But it is finished.
- Shocked and discouraged disciples heard the words and to them it simply meant back to the fishing boats and fishing nets. It is finished.
- Joseph of Arimathea collected the body, wrapped it in some strips of cloth, and put it in a damp tomb. It is finished.

6. Tearing down the cross. During Holy Week at First Presbyterian Church, Orlando Florida, an individual stopped to look at the three crosses that were on display on the front lawn of the church. Enraged at the sight, he tore the center cross down. Repair work began as soon as the church was notified. Damon Willow, one of the associate ministers of the church, looked up at the cross in the midst of repairs and said, "You can tear down the cross, but you can't stop the Christ." The cross is foolishness to some, offensive to others. But to those who have placed faith and trust in the resurrected Lord, it is the power to save.[2]

TEACHING THE BIBLE

- *Main Idea:* Jesus' crucifixion affected people in different ways.
- *Suggested Teaching Aim:* To lead adults to identify different responses to Jesus' death on the cross.

A TEACHING OUTLINE

1. *Crucifixion of Jesus (Matt. 27:32–50)*
2. *Events Following Jesus' Death (Matt. 27:51–61)*

Introduce the Bible Study

Use number 4, "People Like Us," in "Applying the Bible" to introduce the lesson.

Search for Biblical Truth

IN ADVANCE, write the following names on strips of paper and tape them at random around the room: Soldiers (Matt. 27:32–37), Simon of Cyrene (Matt. 27:32–37), Thieves (Matt. 27:38, 44), Passersby (Matt. 27:39, 40), Religious Leaders (Matt. 27:41–43), Resurrected People

(Matt. 27:51–53), Centurion (Matt. 27:54), Women (Matt. 27:55, 56), Joseph of Arimathea (Matt. 27:57–61).

Explain that to understand the cross, we need to see it from the different perspectives of the people involved. Ask members to open their Bibles to Matthew 27:32–37 and skim the verses. Point to *Soldiers* and ask: What was the attitude of the soldiers toward the crucifixion? How did the crucifixion affect them? What lessons can we learn from them? Follow the above procedure with the rest of the names.

Give the Truth a Personal Focus

IN ADVANCE, enlist three readers to read this biblical skit.

Father, Forgive Them

FIRST READER: I hate crucifixions. They are always so messy.

SECOND READER: Yes, and they take so much time. Besides, it's hot out here.

FIRST READER: You shouldn't complain. You were the lucky man with the dice today. You won His robe.

SECOND READER: Look at that! That's the man who was going around saving people! If He is really the Messiah, let Him save Himself now.

FIRST READER: Ha! Save Yourself, O king of the Jews! *(laughs)*

JESUS: "Father, forgive them; for they know not what they do."

SECOND READER: Hey, He's still alive. I wish He were already dead. I'd like to get this over with.

FIRST READER: Look at all those women over there. I wonder what they saw in this guy?

JESUS: "Woman, behold thy son!"

SECOND READER: He was supposed to have a whole group of followers. I don't see but one man in the bunch. I guess what we're doing to their leader put the fear of the gods in them.

JESUS: "Behold thy mother."

FIRST READER: Yeah, but this is such a messy business. I never have liked it.

SECOND READER: Oh, come now, he's just a Jew. He's not even a Roman citizen.

FIRST READER: I know, but He just doesn't look like a criminal. Have you looked into His eyes?

SECOND READER: *That's* your problem. Never look into a condemned man's eyes. The eyes will get you every time.

FIRST READER: But He's not even cursing like the other two. One filthy dog spat right in my face when I was trying to nail his arm. He made it easy for me.

JESUS: "Today shalt thou be with me in paradise."

February 20, 2000

SECOND READER: Well, don't ever look at their eyes. By the way, we're supposed to get this over with before sundown.

FIRST READER: Yeah, it's some kind of religious holiday. These Jews have some kind of dumb law about not having criminals on the cross over a holiday.

SECOND READER: As far as I'm concerned, they have a lot of strange laws. I'll be glad when I'm through with this tour. I'll be glad to get back to Rome.

FIRST READER: I wish my tour had ended before this. I tell you, I don't like it. Something is different about this one.

SECOND READER: Well, I'll admit that when everything went dark and stayed that way for three hours, I felt a little uncomfortable too.

FIRST READER: He just seems so different. I wish I weren't involved in this one.

JESUS: "I thirst."

FIRST READER: Hey, He's thirsty. You might as well give Him a drink of that cheap wine over there. That's the least we can do for the poor fellow.

SECOND READER: Well, it will soon be over. Get that mallet that we drove the spikes with. We need to break their legs.

FIRST READER: I hate to do that. I'd rather let that dirty dog who spat in my face suffer a while.

SECOND READER: I'd like to let them all suffer. Maybe that would teach these Jews that they can't mess with Caesar.

FIRST READER: But He didn't do anything against Caesar. You heard Pilate himself say that He was innocent.

JESUS: "It is finished!"

SECOND READER: Listen! Did you hear Him cry out? It sounded like a cry of victory!

JESUS: "Father, into thy hands I commend my Spirit."

FIRST READER: He looks like He's dead.

SECOND READER: Good. We won't have to break His legs.

FIRST READER: You know, I really believe He was the Son of God.[3]

---

1. Dorothy L. Sayers, "The Man Born to Be King," *Christianity Today*.
2. Howard Edington, *Downtown Church, the Heart of the City* (Nashville: Abingdon Press, 1996), 39.
3. James E. Taulman, *Help! I Need an Idea* (Nashville: Broadman Press, 1987), 42–44.

Resurrection and Commission

February
27
2000

Background Passage: Matthew 27:62–28:20
Focal Passages: Matthew 28:1–10, 16–20

All the New Testament accounts of Jesus' resurrection are distinctive in some ways, but all emphasize the same basic facts: (1) The disciples were not expecting Jesus to be raised from the dead, in spite of all His predictions, (2) the tomb was empty, (3) Jesus appeared alive to many individuals and groups, and (4) the risen Lord commissioned His followers to tell the whole world about the risen Lord. Matthew 28 mentions two of the appearances, and it emphasizes the Great Commission.

▶ **Study Aim:** *To explain how obedience to the Great Commission testifies to a person's faith in the risen Lord.*

STUDYING THE BIBLE

OUTLINE AND SUMMARY
I. Empty Tomb and Risen Lord (Matt. 27:62–28:15)
  1. The sealed tomb (27:62–66)
  2. The empty tomb (28:1–8)
  3. The risen Lord (28:9, 10)
  4. A conspiracy of lies (28:11–15)
II. The Commission of the Risen Lord (Matt. 28:16–20)
  1. Responses to the risen Lord (28:16, 17)
  2. The Great Commission (28:18–20)

The enemies of Jesus sealed His tomb and stationed guards (27:62–66). When women came to the tomb, an angel told them to go tell the disciples that Jesus had been raised from the dead (28:1–8). On their way, they encountered the risen Lord (28:9, 10). When the guards reported what had happened, they accepted a bribe to say that the disciples stole Jesus' body (28:11–15). When Jesus appeared to the disciples in Galilee, they worshiped; but some doubted (28:16, 17). The risen Lord commissioned His followers to make disciples of all nations (28:18–20).

I. Empty Tomb and Risen Lord (Matt. 27:62–28:15)
1. The sealed tomb (27:62–66)
The religious leaders asked Pilate to seal the tomb and station guards (27:62–64a). They wanted to be sure the disciples did not steal the body of Jesus and then claim that He had been raised from the dead (27:64b). After Pilate gave permission, the religious leaders posted guards (27:65, 66).

2. The empty tomb (28:1–8)
> **1** In the end of the sabbath, as it began to dawn toward the first day of the week, came Mary Magdalene and the other Mary to see the sepulchre.

February 27, 2000

As we study the sequence of events about the crucifixion and resurrection of Jesus, three days of the week are mentioned. "The day of the preparation" (27:62) was the Jewish way of describing Friday, the day of preparation for the sabbath, our Saturday. Jesus was crucified between 9:00 A.M. and 3:00 P.M. on Friday of Passover week. He was buried late that day, before sunset, which was the beginning of the Jewish sabbath. The wording of Matthew 28:1 is ambiguous enough to refer either to just after dark on what we would call Saturday or about dawn on Sunday. Luke 24:1 and John 20:1 clearly set the action early on Sunday morning.

According to Matthew 28:1, the two women who came were the same two mentioned in Matthew 27:61, watching the burial of Jesus' body. Mark 16:1 adds Salome to the list.

> **2 And, behold, there was a great earthquake: for the angel of the Lord descended from heaven, and came and rolled back the stone from the door, and sat upon it.**
>
> **3 His countenance was like lightning, and his raiment white as snow:**
>
> **4 And for fear of him the keepers did shake, and became as dead men.**

The information in Matthew 28:2–4 is found only in Matthew's Gospel. None of the Gospels describe the actual resurrection, but verse 2 describes how the angel of the Lord came down and rolled away the stone. The angel's actions and appearance terrified the guards so much that they fell down like dead men. The women had been worried about how they would roll away the stone (Mark 16:3), but they found the stone rolled away and an angel sitting on it.

> **5 And the angel answered and said unto the women, Fear not ye: for I know that ye seek Jesus, which was crucified.**
>
> **6 He is not here: for he is risen, as he said. Come, see the place where the Lord lay.**
>
> **7 And go quickly, and tell his disciples that he is risen from the dead; and, behold, he goeth before you into Galilee; there shall ye see him: lo, I have told you.**
>
> **8 And they departed quickly from the sepulchre with fear and great joy; and did run to bring his disciples word.**

As was often the case when an angel appeared to humans, the angel tried to calm their fears. The angel told the women that he knew that they had come seeking Jesus, who had been crucified and whose body had been placed in this tomb. Quickly the angel told them that the tomb was empty because Jesus had been raised from the dead.

Notice the words "as he said." The angel reminded the women that Jesus had predicted not only His crucifixion but also His resurrection. Looking back from the safe distance of history, we wonder why none of His followers were expecting Jesus to be raised from the dead. The women had not gone to the tomb to see the risen Lord, but to anoint His body (Mark 16:1; Luke 24:1). The disciples did not believe the first reports of His resurrection; they had to see Him for themselves.

The most likely reason why they were not expecting His resurrection is that they had not really expected Him to suffer and die. When Jesus earlier had predicted His suffering, death, and resurrection, the minds of His followers never got past the first part of the prediction.

The angel invited the women to come and see the place where Jesus' body had been. Then the angel told them to go and tell the disciples that Jesus had been raised from the dead. Like a shepherd going ahead of his sheep, Jesus was going ahead of them to Galilee, where they would see Him. The wording did not rule out earlier appearances in Judea (see Luke 24:36–43; John 20:19–29), but it focused attention on the appearance described in Matthew 28:16–20.

The women quickly obeyed the angel. Their fears were not totally gone, but they were now overshadowed by their joy. They ran to tell the disciples the joyful news. Their instant obedience is a model for us who have received the Great Commission.

3. The risen Lord (28:9, 10)

9 And as they went to tell his disciples, behold, Jesus met them, saying, All hail. And they came and held him by the feet, and worshipped him.

10 Then said Jesus unto them, Be not afraid: go tell my brethren that they go into Galilee, and there shall they see me.

One of the many evidences that the New Testament is true is that no one in the first century would have made up a story in which women were the first to see the angel, meet the risen Lord, and tell others. Just as Matthew broke precedent at the beginning of the Gospel by naming women in the genealogy of Jesus (Matt. 1:3, 5, 6), so did he emphasize the crucial role of women as the first to see the Lord alive and to tell that good news to others.

Their initial response was to grasp Jesus about His feet and worship Him. Like the angel, Jesus told them not to be afraid. He also reinforced the command to go and tell the disciples that the Lord would appear to them in Galilee.

4. A conspiracy of lies (28:11–15)

Meanwhile, some of the terrified guards reported to the chief priests what had happened (28:11). The religious leaders bribed the guards to say that the disciples had stolen the body of Jesus while they slept (28:12–14). The guards accepted the bribe and thus began the first of many subsequent ways of trying to explain away the resurrection of Jesus (28:15).

II. The Commission of the Risen Lord (Matt. 28:16–20)

1. Responses to the risen Lord (28:16, 17)

16 Then the eleven disciples went away into Galilee, into a mountain where Jesus had appointed them.

17 And when they saw him, they worshipped him: but some doubted.

February 27, 2000

Matthew mentions only the eleven disciples, but some Bible students think that other believers also could have heard the Great Commission. Jesus certainly did not intend to confine this mission to the apostles.

One reason some people assume that others were present are the words "but some doubted." Some people wonder how the disciples could have doubted, especially if this appearance came near the end of the forty days between the resurrection and the ascension. We do know that the disciples did not believe the first report of the women (Luke 24:11). Thomas thus was not the only doubter. When Jesus appeared to them, their initial responses included fear and uncertainty (Luke 24:36–38). Even after Jesus reassured them, their joy was mixed with some unbelief (Luke 24:41). The Gospels emphasize their honest doubts to show that they became believers only after they saw Him and became totally convinced that it was Jesus raised from the dead.

2. The Great Commission (28:18–20)

> 18 And Jesus came and spake unto them, saying, All power is given unto me in heaven and in earth.
>
> 19 Go ye therefore, and teach all nations, baptizing them in the name of the Father, and of the Son, and of the Holy Ghost:
>
> 20 Teaching them to observe all things whatsoever I have commanded you: and, lo, I am with you alway, even unto the end of the world.

The risen Lord has authority over all things as a result of the successful completion of His mission. This authority has not been openly asserted as it will be at His future coming, but believers already believe He is Lord of all, before whom some day every knee shall bow (Phil. 2:9–11). As Lord of all the earth, Jesus issued a command that encompasses all people. He commissioned His followers to make disciples of people of all nations.

During Jesus' ministry, He sometimes told people not to tell anyone (Matt. 9:30). Even after Peter confessed Jesus as the Christ, Jesus told the disciples not to tell (Matt. 16:20). He was afraid that the Jews of His day would see Him as only an earthly king. By contrast, after His death and resurrection, Jesus issued marching orders for His followers to make disciples of all nations.

Matthew 28:18–20 is called the Great Commission, because it is the fullest statement of the commission for world missions and evangelism. All the Gospels and the Book of Acts have some form of a commission spoken by the risen Lord (see Mark 16:15; Luke 24:47, 48; John 20:21; Acts 1:8).

The word translated "teach" in verse 19 is a different word than "teaching" in verse 20. The meaning in verse 19 is "make disciples." This is the main verb in the Great Commission. Three participles point to three aspects of making disciples. We are to make disciples by going, baptizing, and teaching.

"Go" is translated as a command, and this may be the force of the participle; or it may mean "as you go." Both are true. Sometimes we are called to go to certain places or people. Always we are to bear witness for Christ as we go about our tasks in daily life.

"Baptizing" assumes that those being baptized are people who have heard the good news and have trusted Jesus as Lord and Savior.

"Teaching" is the usual word for Jesus teaching the disciples and for instruction in the early church. This crucial aspect of the Great Commission reminds us that new believers need to be taught about Jesus and His teachings concerning how His followers are to live and serve.

To those who obey this Great Commission, Jesus promises His abiding presence until the end time arrives and His kingdom comes in all its glory. By His Spirit, the risen Lord is leading the way to make disciples of all nations. Our obedience in fulfilling the Great Commission bears testimony to our belief in His resurrection.

PRONUNCIATION GUIDE

Salome   [suh LOH mih]

SUMMARY OF BIBLE TRUTHS

1. The resurrection was the climax of Jesus' earthly mission.
2. The apostles were not expecting His resurrection.
3. They had to be convinced by seeing Him alive.
4. The Great Commission is to make disciples of all nations.
5. Making disciples involves going, baptizing believers, and teaching them the things Jesus wants them to know.
6. The risen Lord promises to be with those who follow Him in fulfilling this commission.

Quotations of the Other Commissions

"Go ye into all the world, and preach the gospel to every creature" (Mark 16:15).

"Repentance and remission of sins should be preached in his name among all nations, beginning at Jerusalem. And ye are witnesses of these things" (Luke 24:47, 48).

"As my Father hath sent me, even so send I you" (John 20:21).

"Ye shall receive power, after that the Holy Ghost is come upon you: and ye shall be witnesses unto me both in Jerusalem, and in all Judaea, and in Samaria, and unto the uttermost part of the earth" (Acts 1:8).

APPLYING THE BIBLE

1. In Jesus' words. "It should ever be remembered that our Lord is never recorded as speaking of His coming cross without at the same time foretelling His resurrection" (G. Campbell Morgan).

2. Hope. Among the earliest manifestations of Christian art are the early third-century paintings of biblical figures on catacomb walls in Rome. Among the main themes portrayed are the hope of resurrection and immortality, symbolized by fish and peacock motifs.[1] From earliest

February 27, 2000

days, it seems the Christian community has held on to the promise of the empty tomb.

3. Why we need hope. Peter Anderheggen became the first subscriber to a magazine called *Hope*. He told reporters, "We don't live without hope." He went on to predict, "The magazine will be successful because it demands us to look at things that do not naturally come to mind as hopeful."[2]

We don't live without hope. We certainly don't stand at the graveside of a loved one without hope. Things that do not naturally come to mind as hopeful have become transformed by the resurrection of Christ.

4. Easter's promise. No matter how bad things may seem, resurrection Sunday reminds us that things are going to get better.

5. Hope in our grief. "The most enduring emblems of tragedy often are poignantly impermanent," writes Mary Lord in an article in *U.S. News & World Report*. When employees of a Starbucks coffee shop were killed, chalk tributes to the three coworkers were lovingly etched on the sidewalk by a member of the community.[3]

6. Conspiracy. Sentinels of the Tomb of the Unknowns officially began guarding the tomb in 1948. But their story began shortly after World War I. The sentinels are held to some of the highest standards in the Army. Their training is rigorous, including about nine months of drilling exercises aimed at near-perfect expertise. They guard the tomb twenty-four hours a day, seven days a week.[4]

The soldiers who were sent to guard the tomb of Jesus were among Rome's best. Skilled and trained, they knew the significance of their task and the penalty that awaited them for failure. Yet it was impossible to stop the resurrection. These soldiers went from being among the elite to becoming part of a cover-up conspiracy.

7. The Great Commission. According to the 1995–96 Annual Church Profile of the Southern Baptist Convention, 10,713 churches reported no baptisms in the previous twelve months. The reason for this boils down to one simple fact: we have forgotten the urgency of the Great Commission. It is the only strategy Christ gave to the church. When we fail to participate in making disciples, we participate in the "Great Omission." Edmund Burke said it accurately: "The only thing necessary for the triumph of evil is for good men to do nothing."

TEACHING THE BIBLE

- *Main Idea:* Our obedience in fulfilling the Great Commission bears testimony to our belief in Jesus' resurrection.
- *Suggested Teaching Aim:* To lead adults to examine how their obedience to the Great Commission reflects their belief in Jesus' resurrection.

A TEACHING OUTLINE

1. Empty Tomb and Risen Lord (Matt. 27:62—28:15)
2. The Commission of the Risen Lord (Matt. 28:16–20)

February 27 2000

Introduce the Bible Study

IN ADVANCE, make a poster of number 4, "Easter's Promise" in "Applying the Bible." Display this and read it to begin the lesson.

Search for Biblical Truth

Ask a member to read silently Matthew 27:62–28:10 and find the three days of the week that are mentioned.

Ask, What was the purpose of the earthquake? (To let people into the tomb, not to let Jesus out.) What was symbolic about the angel sitting on the stone? What was the angel's first word to the women? Can you think of another time this same word was used by an angel? (Luke 2:10.) Why were the women not expecting Him to be raised? (They hadn't expected Him to die.) Was it only coincidental that the women met Jesus as they obeyed the angel's message to go tell the disciples Jesus was alive?

DISCUSS: Do you see anything significant in women being the first messengers of the resurrection? How had Matthew emphasized women in the genealogy of Jesus? (Matt. 1:3, 5, 6.) Are these two purposes related?

Ask members to scan Matthew 28:16–20. Ask: Why would anyone doubt Jesus was alive? Where did Jesus get His power over all things?

On a chalkboard write *make disciples* ("teach" [v. 19] in KJV). Point out that making disciples is the primary objective of the Great Commission. Ask members to examine verses 19–20 to find three ways Christ's followers are to make disciples. (Go, baptize, teach.) Ask, What is the wonderful promise He gives us as we make disciples?

Give the Truth a Personal Focus

Read number 7, "The Great Commission," in "Applying the Bible." Ask: Does your obedience to the Great Commission reflect your belief in Christ's resurrection. If we do not make disciples, do we really believe Christ is alive? Close in prayer that members will make disciples as they go to their separate worlds of work this week.

---

1. *The Concise Columbia Encyclopedia* (Columbia University Press, 1989, 1991).
2. Cheryl Wetzstein, "Always Hope for the Best," *Insight on the News,* April 15, 1996, 38.
3. Mary Lord, "Finding a Way to Grieve," *U.S. News & World Report,* July 28, 1997, 16.
4. Tranette Ledford, "Tomb Sentinels Mark 50th Anniversary," *Army Times,* March 8, 1998.